A lad from Donke

A Rugby League ...

Austin Rhodes

London League Publications Ltd

A lad from Donkey Common
A Rugby League life

A CIP catalogue record for this book is available from the British Library.

First published in Great Britain in September 2012 by:
London League Publications Ltd, P.O. Box 65784, London NW2 9NS

ISBN:	978-1903659-64-9
Cover design by:	Stephen McCarthy Graphic Design
46, Clarence Road, London N15 5BB
Layout:	Peter Lush

Printed and bound in Great Britain by Charlesworth Press, Wakefield

Foreword

I've known Austin Rhodes for many years and I played against him before we lined up in our first international together. My impression always was that he was quite some player. If you look at the records, he could play at full-back, centre and in both half-back positions. I can't recall many who could do that and do it as well as he did. Mind you, if they'd have asked him to play prop forward I think he would have done. I believe that he should have got more caps than he did too.

We were both in the victorious World Cup winning side and neither of us was guaranteed a place initially. There was a squad of 18 players and we both came through in the end. As it happened, Austin got the full-back berth and I was stand-off. It was very physical and obviously against any Australian side you just had to be on your mettle. We were only kids and very nervous, but we came through and did our jobs in the end.

From being team-mates at international level and opponents with our respective clubs, we were re-united again when I was at Saints in the late 1960s. Joe Coan was coach then and I remember him coming over to me during one training session and he asked my advice about Austin Rhodes coming back to St Helens. I said that there was no question in my mind that the club should go for him. Even though he was at the latter end of his career he still had some great games when he came back to Knowsley Road.

As a person, Austin is very much an easy going sort of lad, very witty and remains a good friend. We have also played a lot of golf together and our families still meet up socially.

Frank Myler
Widnes, St Helens, Rochdale Hornets, Lancashire,
England and Great Britain

Photo courtesy Robert Gate

Acknowledgements

To write a life story such as this requires a great deal of help and co-operation from so many people and I would like to thank everyone who made this book come to life. If I have left anyone out it is certainly not intentional.

Frank Myler for the foreword; Brian Cahill; Tommy Bracken; Wilf Smith; Denis Whittle; Glyn Moses; Brian Howard; Dick Huddart; Billy Boston; Brian McGinn; Jimmy Measures; Bev Risman; Billy Benyon; John Forster; Geoff Pimblett; Roger Grime; John Riding and the one and only Tom van Vollenhoven for The last word.

Statistics: Bill Bates and Alex Service [see the Saints' Heritage Society's website www.saints.org.uk]

Images: Unless indicated, the bulk of images are provided by Saints' Historian Alex Service. Special thanks to Karen Rhodes; Abe Terry; Curtis Johnstone; *St Helens Reporter*; St Helens Local History Library; Harry Edgar (*Rugby League Journal*); Robert Gate; Bernard Platt and St Helens RLFC.

Special Thanks:

Alex Service for all his help and support.
Geoff Pimblett and the St Helens Players Association.
Peter Lush and Dave Farrar at London League Publications for their interest and help.
Geoff Lee – a big fan!

Research: St Helens Local History Library.

I could not have managed this book without the tremendous encouragement from my wife, Marlene, son Martyn and daughter Karen. I would also like to give a special mention to Alex Service and Denis Whittle. Alex has an amazing knowledge of the game of rugby league and whenever I had any doubts about my memory letting me down I could always rely on him to correct me.

Austin Rhodes October 2011

Contents

Prologue – I owe it all to rugby

I was born in St Helens on 25 February 1937, not a particularly good time, some may say, with the world about to be shrouded under the clouds of war. Rations and blackouts would become the norm after 1939. Yet the year of 1937 did produce a new King, George VI, and a new Prime Minister, Neville 'Peace in our time' Chamberlain. Further research (on the internet, of course) tells me that I share an exact birth date with the actor Tom Courtenay, who found fame with his roles in *The Loneliness of the Long Distance Runner* and *Doctor Zhivago*. There was the Hindenburg airship disaster that same year; the Golden Gate Bridge in California was opened and Sir Frank Whittle tested the first jet engine – on the ground I should add.

Some of the famous people who were also born in 1937 include Bobby Charlton, the great footballer; actress Jane Fonda – I fancied her; Morgan Freeman, the great actor – I think the world of him; and Joe Louis, who is my favourite boxer, along with Sugar Ray Robinson and Randolph Turpin. My favourite comic, *The Dandy*, was also first published in 1937, so it must have been a special year.

In my life sport has been one major thread – and rugby league in particular. It has shaped my destiny. Just to be a member of the first St Helens team to win the Challenge Cup in 1956 was an awesome experience. To beat Wigan at Wembley five years later and wear the red vee jersey for the first time was equally a magical achievement. Yet I was also able to enjoy the ultimate accolade of being a member of the Great Britain team which won the World Cup in 1960. It doesn't get any better.

As a result of rugby league I was able to meet my wife, buy my house and forge enduring friendships with many people at home and abroad. Perhaps I have paid the price for competing in such a tough professional sport as rugby league with a series of hip replacements over the years since I retired from playing. I have had four procedures on the same hip up to 2011 – probably a world record. But if I had my time again would I change anything? Not really. In the following pages I have tried my best to chronicle my sporting odyssey and my life in general, with maybe one or two surprises along the way. Not bad for a lad from Donkey Common, or to the uninitiated, Thatto Heath.

Austin Rhodes

1. A lad from Donkey Common

"We were in the same class at St Austin's school all the way through. Austin lived on the Dam Bank, whereas I lived in Sunbury Street. Austin played stand-off and I played scrum-half in the school team until I left and Alex Murphy took over. We used to walk home together after school. Austin's house was posh – he had a toilet inside. He was a great rugby league player, but very much an all-round athlete. He was great at soccer and cricket as well. Thatto Heath was a fantastic place to grow up in. Our headmaster at school, Gerry Landers was brilliant – very eccentric. He loved his rugby too. We thought the world of him. Later, Austin and I used to go in the old St Austin's club after church. When it closed for drinking, the steward would let us stay on and have a game of billiards. Austin carried on with his rugby after school, but I had my apprenticeship to do. They were difficult days growing up after the war, but we survived and definitely made the most of it."
Brian Cahill
Classmate St Austin's School, Thatto Heath

Apparently my family name is quite an old one, Anglo-Saxon in origin and found chiefly in Lancashire and Yorkshire. It can be a topographical name for someone who lived by a clearing in woodland. The old English word 'rod' actually means a clearing. Either that or it relates to a particular location with 'rod' in it, like the place name Rhodes in Lancashire. I'm not sure about it in my case, with my mother having Irish blood in her veins; my father Welsh, though not directly. Our particular 'clearing' was a district of St Helens called Thatto Heath, also known colloquially as Donkey Common. Wedged in between the other districts of West Park, Eccleston Park and Nutgrove it has its own distinct character and characters. There was a great variety of people who brought the place to life every day, especially the miners walking home after their shift with their clogs and blackened faces. In many ways we were Thatto Heath first, St Helens second. The area has a large Catholic community. I thought it was a great place to grow up in and there was something for everyone. It was quite rare that we actually needed to go into St Helens for anything.

I lived with my mum and dad and uncle, Jack Greenall, on Thatto Heath Road, in a semi-detached house opposite Bates Crescent and

Thatto Heath Park. Thatto Heath Road is a busy main road linking Thatto Heath with St Helens in one direction and Rainhill in the other. The house is part of a row of 1930s semi-detached houses from the bottom of Toll Bar to what is now a car wash. There are no houses opposite. That is the area of Thatto Heath Park, a place we used to call 'God's little acre,' wedged in between Elm Road, Thatto Heath Road and the railway line that links St Helens with Liverpool in one direction and Wigan and Preston in the other. There is a small station further up the road on our side called Thatto Heath.

My father, Jack, worked down the pit at Lea Green colliery all his working life and my mother, Agnes, finished work at Rainhill Psychiatric Hospital when I was born. All the Greenall side of the family worked at the Hospital and all the Rhodes side of the family, apart from my father. Our house backed on to a small man-made lake called Thatto Heath Dam, which belonged to the Pilkington family. Of course this was supposed to be strictly out of bounds and fishing was illegal. That didn't matter to us as kids though. There was a warden, known as 'Old Joe' but we used to be warned well in advance when he was coming and I only had to roll down the grass bank and I was in our back garden. As soon as Old Joe had gone everyone went back to fishing for roach, perch and carp.

Like everyone born in the late 1930s, we would shortly experience what it was like living with war. Although St Helens received very little attention from the German Luftwaffe, despite being an important industrial town, I can distinctly remember the police knocking on our front door to tell us to close the blinds on our front window because the blackout was in force. Along with other families during the war we had our own hens. We would collect the eggs in the morning ready for cooking later in the day.

When hostilities ceased in 1945, we had a huge celebratory bonfire on some spare land close to us and all stayed up until the early hours making jacket potatoes in the ashes of the fire. They were absolutely delicious.

My uncle Jack lived with us. He was a rum bugger. My mum and dad were in one bedroom, Uncle Jack in the other and I had the smaller box room. I woke up one morning and I heard a large bump. He had got in at 3am from Rainhill Ex-Services Club having had a skin-full of ale. He collapsed on the landing as dead as a dodo outside my bedroom. I was used to looking at dead bodies. I was an altar boy and, in those days, the coffin was often open before being carried to the altar, so I wasn't that shocked.

However, Jack Greenall had been a decent crown green bowler and everybody knew him around Thatto Heath. Jack would, of course, do a lot of bowling in Thatto Heath Park. There was also a pub next to the park, called the Alexandra Hotel, which also had a superb bowling green, but for me, the bowling matches at Thatto Heath Park took some beating. They were deadly serious. I used to go with my parents about half an hour before the start otherwise we wouldn't get a view of the proceedings. The atmosphere was electric with some of the best bowlers in the county playing, such as Frank Waterworth, Jimmy Foulkes – the father of Bill who played for Manchester United, 'Naily' Pennington and Bob Gee to name a few. The biggest battle of all was always between Foulkes and Waterworth. Foulkes was the 'baddy' and Waterworth the 'goody' it seemed to me. When Waterworth got a lucky deflection Foulkes would go over to him and ask him if he had been to church that morning and all the Catholics in the crowd would go mad, including my mother.

For kids growing up, Thatto Heath Park was a fantastic place. I spent many days there in the school holidays in particular. There were two tennis courts, two bowling greens and a large area of grass behind where there was more than enough room to play huge games of tick rugby or football. On a weekend it was very often a game of tick rugby between the married and single men. The single men nearly always won because the married men were more often than not a little bit 'worse for wear' after coming out of the Vine Tavern.

There was the railway line, of course, behind the park and I was one of many young boys who took train numbers at Thatto Heath station, which was a huge pastime in itself in those days. Whenever a train came into the station, the whole place would be submerged by a giant cloud of steam. Near the park were the mushroom fields. I remember going camping there one time and I didn't enjoy the experience in the least. I ended knocking up my parents at about 2am and explaining that perhaps this camping lark wasn't for me.

About 40 yards from the station was one of the area's most famous landmarks, the Empire Cinema, known locally as the 'Emp'. In my younger days I spent many a happy Saturday afternoon in the old place watching cowboy films starring Roy Rogers, 'Wild Bill' Hickok and comedies with Bud Abbott and Lou Costello. Yet one of the best laughs of all was when someone pushed the cinema cat off the balcony onto the patrons below. There was a guy called Les whose job it was to keep order in the queues before the film began and he was probably the first bouncer I remember.

I went to a school called St Austin's, off Scholes Lane and in easy walking distance from home. My days in the infants, in particular, were very happy indeed. As I will recall in some detail further on sport was so important in Thatto Heath and it produced such a fierce sense of competitiveness among us, whether for our schools, local junior clubs or just playing in the park. It didn't matter what we played: rugby, soccer, cricket; there was tremendous rivalry and we always wanted to win. In fact, they always used to say they never did the three 'Rs' at St Austin's. It was just the two − rugby league and religion.

One big attraction twice a year in Thatto Heath was Silcock's Fair on the Mushroom Fields, as we used to call them, next to Thatto Heath Park. They used to have boxing and all-in wrestling. I saw some good scraps there. Lads would fancy their chances at beating one of the semi-pros in the boxing ring. If you could last a couple of rounds you would get, say, ten bob [50p]. Freddie Leyland, a ginger-haired lad who trained me when I was with the Thatto Heath team in the Continuation League, for players aged 15 to 16, always fancied his chances. He was a good boxer too. Freddie had played on the wing for Salford before he came to coach us, so he was no slouch either. I remember one of my heroes, Jonty Pilkington of Saints fame, slugging it out with a pro and going the distance, much to everyone's delight except the so-called professional that is.

Apparently there were even more important things in life. I come from a strong Catholic family. My mum and dad were devout Catholics and persuaded me to learn Latin and to be an altar boy at St Austin's church. I did so and went to Mass and Holy Communion nearly every day before going to school. We had a piano in our house and many other houses had them in those days. As a result I learnt to play the piano from quite an early age. Both my parents were musical in their own way and were both regulars in the choir at St Austin's Church. Dad was a tenor, who used to listen to the records of the Italian opera singer Beniamino Gigli, while mum was a soprano of repute. I had

4

formal lessons with Miss Boyson in Roby Street, near Prescot Road, twice a week and I managed to pass loads of music exams. I used to have to go to Rushworths and Draper in Liverpool to take the exams. We were judged on a set musical piece. I only needed one more grade to qualify for my 'cap and gown' which meant, in effect that I could have taught music. It wasn't necessarily a 'social' thing – just a desire to get through the exams.

I never played music that suited the lads. When we were on a trip say for a cup match they would say 'Come on Rhodesey, give us a tune.' Now I was more concerned with passing my next exam, so things like *Roll out the Barrel* and suchlike was quite alien to me. I don't think that the lads would have really appreciated what I would have played for them. I could read music, but I didn't have an ear for it. I had to have a sheet in front of me. I couldn't make something up or anything like that. When I later signed for Saints, my musical career effectively ceased.

The place for all seasons

Overall, my childhood was wonderful, full of excitement, opportunity and adventure. We didn't need the likes of Alton Towers or Disneyland in those days. As if Thatto Heath Park wasn't enough, we used to walk up Lugsmore Lane to Toll Bar, cross Prescot Road and there was another magnificent park for us. Taylor Park was a fantastic place too and had everything a youngster needed – truly a place for all seasons. In spring we would feed the swans and ducks, together with their youngsters on the Big Lake. The older lads would tell us not to go near the swans at this time of the year because they could break your leg with one swipe of their wing. I never actually saw it happen but it was definitely not worth taking the risk.

There was an aviary in the sandstone quarry nearby which was alive with all types of birds, rabbits and guinea pigs. If someone was really adventurous they could climb their way out of the aviary up the old quarry walls. If they were 'soft' they could always walk round. The rhododendron bushes were ablaze with colour and it was always a great place to play hide and seek.

Summer was just a magical time. It always seemed as though the weather was better then, but I'm sure it could be my imagination playing tricks. The boats were out on the lake and we could row round and round until our number was called out. We never did find out how deep the lake was in the middle, but people used to say it was bottomless. I swam the lake on many occasions; sometimes with Saints' Welsh centre Don Gullick. He often used to have his son David on his back, which I thought was a bit risky but it proved to be no problem, given his father's incredible strength. Don was a great man, a good friend and someone for whom I had a great deal of respect.

To see the lake in more leisurely fashion and if we had two old pence we could go on Taylor Park's very own Queen Mary. Somebody told me that she was sunk in the middle of the lake when she came to the end of her working life. There was also a smaller paddling pool, which was the place to be on a boiling hot summer's day. Kids would be sailing their little boats, with a lolly in one hand and a towel in the other. Sheer heaven.

In autumn we all went fishing in the Big Lake for perch and pike. One of the pike apparently was so big that it used to swallow the young ducklings whole, long before *Jaws* was ever heard of. There were some big pike in there but I must admit I never caught one. Just down the road was the Leg o' Mutton dam where once again we used to fish to our heart's content.

Winter was best. Once the snow got on the 'big hill' we wouldn't get in before 10pm. It was a case of how many people we could get on one sledge and still be able to steer. We used to see who could clear the bandstand or crash the hardest into the bushes at the bottom. It's a wonder that someone didn't get seriously hurt, but we didn't care. Every possible contraption was used as a sledge. Come February I don't think there was a tray left in any house for miles around. Eventually we did need to make our way home – soaking wet, freezing cold and tired out, but so happy. You can keep your computers, mobile phones and games consoles. How can they ever compare to the wonders of a place like Taylor Park?

Coming of age

I left St Austin's School aged 15, and at the age of 16 I started work as an apprentice toolmaker at Ashdown's, a subsidiary of Pilkington Brothers, which later became Triplex. I would ride my bicycle from

Thatto Heath Road through Taylor Park and clock on for 8am at the factory. Coming out of my teenage years there were different leisure activities to savour. Apart from the nearby Thatto Heath Empire cinema, there seemed to be a pub around every corner in Thatto Heath. There was the British Lion, where the licensee was a big Saints fan called Alec Service, at the bottom of Toll Bar, The Springfield on Thatto Heath Road, which was run by George Wright – a Liverpool FC diehard, and The Alexandra Hotel in Crossley Road next to the park whose landlord was Dave Kidd – a retired police inspector. There was also the legendary Vine Tavern on Elephant Lane run by Frank Bowen who played for St Helens Recs and was an England [Great Britain] tourist in 1928 and The Elephant Hotel, run by Harry Hampton, although I didn't go there that much. We used to go a bit further away for a pint or two when we got older and ended up in the Boar's Head in Sutton Heath. One of my best mates at the time was a lad called Brian Cahill, whose elder brother Ted went on the 1954 rugby league tour to Australasia.

It would be remiss of me if I didn't mention the legendary 'Whisper' Leyland. People called him 'Whisper' because of his big booming voice. Basically he was famous for his ability to drink massive quantities of beer, and often went to Prescot, Billinge and even Wigan on a challenge to who could drink the most beer. I used to watch him many times in the Vine Tavern and wondered where he managed to put it all.

Pitch and toss was a regular Sunday afternoon pastime after the pubs had closed at 2pm. This was an illegal activity and some young lads were used as lookouts in case the police came. The boys in blue were only too willing to raid these groups and make arrests. Many an argument broke out and then a fight would ensue after someone had lost a lot of money.

I only really began to venture into St Helens when I started playing for Saints. Then we went to the Co-op in Baldwin Street for Saturday night dances and walked back to Thatto Heath. It was a demanding walk when we were full of ale. We had a cat and she was always waiting for me at the top of Toll Bar. I don't know how or why, but she was always there. I'd hear meowing and she'd be there walking behind me; not by the side of me like a dog would. She walked through the gardens of the houses in Lugsmore Lane. I'd talk to her and let her in when I got home. Happy days – and nights – indeed in Thatto Heath.

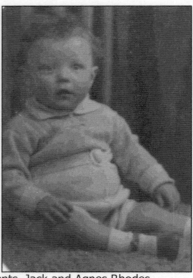

Left: An early photograph of my parents, Jack and Agnes Rhodes.
Right: The archetypal bouncing baby boy – 16 April 1938.

Happy days indeed. Walking on the prom at Blackpool with mum and dad.

2. My early sporting life

'When you first went to St Austin's school the first thing that hit you was that it wasn't sports-mad, but rugby league mad. The headmaster, Gerry Landers, was an Army colleague of Gus Risman's and his love of the game was well known. He was so enthusiastic and wanted the school to do as well as possible. Even before Austin and later, of course, Alex Murphy, the school was producing great players like Ted Cahill, Bernard Dwyer (senior), Peter Metcalfe and Walt Tabern. St Austin's was steeped in rugby league. Despite being a small school, with 200 boys, we always put out teams and competed with the best in the town. When I first arrived there and saw Austin in the top class, a St Helens and Lancashire schoolboy, Everton trialist, I really did look up to him in the sporting sense."

Tommy Bracken
St Austin's schoolboy player

My first memories of rugby league football go back to just after the war. As a 10-year-old, I used to watch the Saints. They were not a particularly good side and were in the shadow of Wigan. St Helens had a great following in those days and my heroes included our centre Jimmy Stott and Jonty Pilkington. Jonty was a 'likable rogue' who did quite a bit of fairground boxing. When he played for the Saints he always seemed to get himself sent off. I was also brought up on tales of second-rower Jack Arkwright, who began his career at St Helens and became a Warrington legend. He went on the Australian tour in 1936 and during one up-country game, he got sent off. Jack sneaked back onto the field and battered another Aussie before the referee realised he should not have been on the field at all.

Then there was Stan McCormick on the wing, formerly of Belle Vue Rangers, who was a real showman, with the ability to pull off many memorable interception tries.

Duggie Greenall was a big favourite too and a real character. Rumour has it that when Duggie toured Australia in 1954, all that he took with him was a spare pair of underpants and an extra shirt in a Marks and Spencer's bag. That was to last him three months in Australia. Duggie became a good friend of mine and after matches on the way home from Cumberland and Yorkshire he used to entertain us with some fabulous renditions of Frank Sinatra and Nat King Cole standards. Duggie also talked a lot about his exploits in the Army but I got it from good authority that he failed his medical as a result of his flat feet.

It was not all rugby league. At the time both my dad and my uncle Billy were big Everton supporters and we would spend one week watching Everton and the other watching Saints. Uncle Billy was very involved with boxing. He had a gym in Prescot and a few professionals used it on occasions. My dad had one or two fights for money in Liverpool but he never won a world championship or anything like that. Only joking, of course, but he did buy me a punch ball which I used every day. I thought that did me a world of good and helped with my timing in later years.

At the school I attended, St Austin's Boys school in Thatto Heath, the game was tantamount to a religion and my headmaster Gerry Landers and all the members of staff were equally fanatical in their approach to the game. Maybe we suffered academically because of our love for sport, but we would never swap rugby practice for study.

Being a very small school with a low intake, St Austin's always had difficulty in fielding 13 fit boys because out of the 30 in the year group, it was inevitable that some had ill health and some didn't have the coordination between mind and muscle to be any good at rugby. Actually, it was quite an achievement in those days for my school to reach a final of the Waring Cup or Ellison Cup considering the disadvantages and problems that existed. The headmaster and his staff had a really 'never-say-die' attitude and regularly turned out teams that were equal and very often superior to far bigger schools.

I would think that between 1947 and 1952, St Austin's were in more finals than they missed and even 'posh' schools like Grange Park and Parr Central must have dreaded playing us on our own midden when all the school and parents turned up to shout for us. Any pupil who was absent from the match got 10 of the best from Gerry the next day.

Just after I was born they built a lot of houses on the Portico and Grange Park estate, including a new secondary school, called Grange Park. When I first played there I thought it was really 'posh' because it was the first time I had a shower. It was heaven. When we played at St Austin's there would be 26 kids, full of slutch, trying to get clean in two wash basins.

10

Daily Dispatch

SCHOOLS' RUGBY LEAGUE SHIELD COMPETITION

•

FINAL

ST. AUSTIN'S

ST. HELENS

versus

ALL SAINTS'

WIGAN

•

Wednesday, 21st May, 1952

on Messrs. Pilkington's Ground, City Road

(by kind permission)

KICK-OFF - 7 p.m.

•

Admission : **ADULTS 6d.**   -   **SCHOLARS 3d.**

Programme for the 1952 *Daily Dispatch* final, which featured four future international half-backs: Rhodes, Murphy, Holden and Bolton.

They were our big rivals. Freddie Hewitt was one of their stars, a superb schoolboy stand-off, who went on to play for Leigh as a full-back. We later became team-mates in the early 1960s when I left Saints. Hooker Bob Dagnall went to Grange Park too, as did Brian Glover, who played for Warrington and St Helens. Ronnie King was a great football player and a fantastic dribbler. Jackie Wood was a big mate of mine and we used to go to the Isle of Man for the TT races, although I used to go for the swimming as much as the bikes. It's such a shame to think that Grange Park has been demolished. St Austin's, too, has been rebuilt and they don't seem to have a rugby league team anymore. Doubtless old Gerry Landers will be turning in his grave.

It wasn't just rugby. I played cricket and football for the school team. I remember playing against another of our great rivals the Council School and we won 3–0. I scored all three goals and when I went into school next day the headmaster Gerry Landers got me to one side and gave me a big lecture about being swollen headed. It was just his way of keeping my feet on the ground. I remember a scout from Everton Football Club coming round the schools in about 1950. He gave me a few exercises to do and asked me to go to Everton for a trial. I thought about it, but decided that rugby was my going to be my sport.

One of my big mates at school was Brian Cahill. Brian was my scrum-half all through St Austin's until the Christmas time and a certain Alex Murphy came along and we played a full season together, even though he was two years younger than me. Before that, the school produced another terrific scrum-half by the name of Tommy Finn, who found fame at Hull. On reflection it is amazing how much alike Tommy and Alex were in their attitudes even at that early age. Our school always produced three or four boys good enough to play in the Town team and also had a long list of county players, but could not produce any cups. It seemed that whenever St Austin's reached a final, Lady Luck turned her back on us, and we finished the day losing by some diabolical refereeing decision or a last-minute drop goal.

One day, we played in the final of the Waring Cup against Grange Park. A lad called Geoff Kelly knocked on about four times but was amazingly awarded a try to rob us of the cup. On another occasion, in the Tom Finn years, I remember Jack Bamber from Parr Central pinched the cup off us with a last-minute drop goal. Perseverance, however, finally paid off. We were to play Rivington at the Saints

12

ground in the final of the Ellison Cup and having beaten them already on two previous occasions, were favourites to win. Things started to go wrong, however, for we were losing 3–0 with five minutes to go. One of our forwards forced his way over and our centre, Jimmy Swift kicked a magnificent goal off the touchline to give us victory. It was a highly emotional occasion. Most of the boys burst into tears and, I suspect, most of the staff did too.

We all went to the Co-op for a celebration tea and I was presented with the cup to mark one of the happiest moments of my life. Also we were half-a-crown better off, thanks to the Saints director Lionel Swift, who dug into his pocket to reward the lads for their achievements. My first professional pay packet. Talking of cash, I can remember to this day the time when I failed my eleven plus exam. Gerry Landers visited our house to sympathise with my parents, but got everything into proportion with his parting words: "Never mind, Austin. Think what a great team we'll have next year," and he gave me another half-a-crown.

Another very happy memory of mine was captaining St Helens Schoolboys in the Lancashire Cup Final, which we won comfortably and again celebrated with a meal at the Co-op.

One of my saddest moments was walking off the City Road pitch after the final of the *Daily Dispatch* Shield in 1952. If we had been successful, it would have made us the champion school of Lancashire. Unfortunately we lost to a much bigger school team – All Saints' from Wigan – who included two future Great Britain players in their line-up. In fact, all four half-backs in that match went on to play professional rugby league for their country. I should imagine that there is a record there somewhere: Austin Rhodes and Alex Murphy from St Austin's and Dave Bolton and Keith Holden from All Saints.

I left school at 15 and was about to start another chapter in my life in which sport was to play a continuing part, but I could never forget those great days at St Austin's and the two 'Rs' – rugby and religion – the best education anyone could ever have in my opinion.

St Austin's line up before the 1951 Ellison Cup final at City Road.

"Thank you, your worship." Receiving the Ellison Cup from the Mayor at the Town Hall on behalf of St Austin's School. Alex Murphy is on the far right.

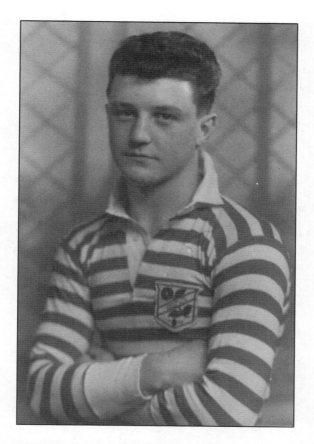

Top: In my Lancashire County schoolboy jersey, aged 14.
Bottom: 'God's Little Acre'. Thatto Heath Park in 1960,
showing the bowling green.

Saints sent me on a training course to Bisham Abbey with other young hopefuls. I am on the back row, far right. Wigan's Dave Bolton is in the centre of the front row.

My other sporting passion. St Helens Schoolboys line up before a match at St Helens Town's ground at Hoghton Road. I am second from the left on the front row. The player second from the right is John Connelly, a future member of England's World Cup squad in 1966.

16

3. Becoming a Saint

"Austin was stand-off in my first-ever 'A' team game at Knowsley Road. It came about because the regular 'A' team scrum-half, Billy Adams, cut his finger off at work. We were in the final of the Lancashire Shield. Billy Mercer was the coach and my boss at the Corporation and asked me if I would play. I was with Clock Face amateurs at the time. We won 14–3 and I think Austin scored all the points. I went on to sign for the Saints and Austin and I went on to play in some fantastic games for the club over the next few years. He was one of the best utility players ever. His individual flair did not alter no matter what position he played in, whether it was full-back, stand-off or centre. Austin was a brilliant attacking full-back, though and a great goalkicker too."
Wilf Smith
St Helens RLFC 1955 to 1969

Although I signed amateur forms for the Saints at 15, I also had a spell where I played football. I was with Toll Bar Congs in the local junior leagues and they were quite successful. I went on to play rugby league for St Austin's in the Continuation League, which had just been formed at under-17 level. This was set up as a bridge between leaving school and the open age teams – otherwise there was nothing. It didn't mean that it was all former St Austin's lads in the team though. We played at Saints' ground in a final and won it. I had attracted the attention of the Saints' directors when I was captain of St Austin's School in the Ellison Cup Final and then I captained the town team in the Lancashire Cup Final, which we also won. I signed for the club just after my 16th birthday and went straight into the 'A' team.

I signed as a professional for the princely sum of £100. The chairman at the time was Harry Cook and he offered me £80 to sign. My dad wanted me to accept £80, but I told Mr Cook that Gus Risman – the coach at Workington – wanted me to sign for them and had offered me £150 for the privilege. The Saints' chairman told us that he would get into trouble with his fellow directors if he was to give any more, but he then offered me £100 and I signed there and then. I subsequently used the same tactic on a few occasions later in my career. In fact, Gus Risman was someone I had read about in the papers and I had never met or spoken to him. But later on I played

17

scrum-half to his son Bev who went on to captain a Great Britain side on tour in Australia which, to my mind, is the greatest honour of all!

Playing in the 'A' team was quite an experience. I had watched many games at Saints and had been in the dressing rooms for schoolboy matches, so it was no big shock in that respect. I can honestly say that I never felt intimidated by the prospect of playing as a professional. There was a real mix in the dressing room. There were some youngsters like me; some players who were regarded as 'stalwarts' of the 'A' team who would get occasional call-ups into the first team and, perhaps those who were getting a bit too old and would be ready to finish their careers elsewhere. Overall I felt confident in my new environment. I could show my ability on the training pitch. I had a natural sidestep from both feet, so I could lead burly forwards a bit of a merry dance. A lot of the forwards couldn't even pass the ball. Mind you, they didn't need to in those days. They concentrated on getting the ball from set scrums and just carting it up in attack.

The 'A' team coach was Billy Mercer, who had played in the same team as Alf Ellaby before the war and was an England international centre. Everyone liked him and he seemed to think that I had the potential to go further in the future. There was no doubt in my mind that I would. One of the stalwarts of the 'A' team was the Australian Max Garbler, who played mostly as a loose-forward. I had a high regard for him as a player. He was a bit of a shouter, but he looked after me in the early days. Perhaps the one thing that was apparent was the tremendous competition for places in both the 'A' and senior teams. In the half-backs there was Billy Adams, Tommy Finn and Joe Ball who were 'A' team regulars. Tommy Finn was a St Austin's pupil, who eventually went to Hull, played in the Challenge Cup Final in 1960 and scored a brilliant try. That try was shown every Saturday for many years afterwards as part of the opening sequence for BBC television's *Grandstand*. Joe Ball was a typical 'pocket battleship' scrum-half, who was as strong as a horse, although he did lack pace. He eventually moved to Barrow. He did play full-back, but his best position was scrum-half.

Competition was strong on the wings too. There was Alec Davies, Frank Carlton, David Johnson and Eric Ledger – all fliers and desperate to depose the first team pairing of Stan McCormick and Steve Llewellyn. At full-back there was Arthur Pimblett, a brilliant goalkicker who eventually joined Widnes. There were people like Bill Boycott, Roy Robinson, Wilf O'Mara, Bill Knowles, Josh Gaskell, Frank McCabe, Len McIntyre, Abe Terry and Billy Blan. Ray Ashby, who won the Lance Todd trophy with Wigan in 1965, also played a few matches for Saints' 'A' team after I did.

Training was on Tuesday and Thursday nights for both 'A' and first teams. We only had the one training area. We did a couple of laps to start with, followed by a few gentle stretching exercise and lots and lots of sprinting on the track – mostly 50 to 60 yard sprints. There was a cinder track round the whole training pitch, but the main sprinting area was near the main entrance next to the railway.

Generally speaking I soon felt as though I was an established member of the 'A' team and I used to go around with the likes of Wilf Smith, 'Todder' Dickinson, Frank Carlton and Eric Ledger after training – all good lads in their own way. Towards the end of the 1954–55 season, the club gave me the chance to show what I could do at top level and I did not want to disappoint them.

A first teamer to stay

My chance came when I was selected for the league match against Liverpool City at Knowsley Road on 28 March 1955. It was a low key affair, with about 8,000 fans present. The team was not going to get into the top four, so I suppose it was an ideal situation to bring a youngster in. I took Peter Metcalfe's place at stand-off, with Todder Dickinson at scrum-half. I played in every game for the remainder of the season, apart from the match against Wigan at Central Park, when Peter Metcalfe came in once more.

Looking back at the team that played against Liverpool City some 56 years later, it is sad to relate that apart from yours truly, Glyn Moses is the only other player still alive. It was not quite a full-strength team, but very capable nonetheless. At full-back, Glyn Moses was as a solid as a rock; not particularly mobile, but as a last line of defence he was right up there with the best. Unlike most full-backs, he was not a kicker of the ball. Bill Finnan was on the right wing, but was more used to a centre or stand-off role. He was my stand-off at Wembley 12 months later. Frank Carlton was on the left flank. He was a real class act, with his smooth running action. During the 1954–55 season he made 36

19

appearances and scored 33 tries. A good defensive winger too, but he used his pace rather than sheer aggression, which Mick Sullivan did. In the centres were Duggie Greenall and Don Gullick, both great blokes to have on your side, but extremely aggressive. I remember leaving the Pavilion at Watersheddings, Oldham with my opposite number Frank Daley next to me. He had quite a reputation himself for being a bruiser. Duggie Greenall was shouting obscenities at him as we walked through the crowd onto the playing area. Then Don Gullick would carry it on: "And when he's finished with you it's my turn." Verbal intimidation would start well before the kick-off.

My partner at scrum-half was Joe Ball, who kicked three goals in the match and was a real tough guy. In the front-row was the skipper, Alan Prescott, who was supremely fit and very much in his pomp. His partner was Eric Ayles, the former Belle Vue Ranger who was a great lad, but a real tough bugger on the field. Hooker Pat Lannon scored a try in my debut match and was another stalwart of the first team during the season with 38 matches under his belt. George Parsons was one second-rower, a big lad who had great hands and quite a bit of pace. He scored Saints' second try against Liverpool City. Nat Silcock was the other, who had joined St Helens from Wigan during the season. A fabulous player, Nat had it all – not a great defender as such, but he had electrifying pace and a jack-hammer hand-off. He was a big lad too, over 16 stones. Finally, at loose-forward, was Billy Blan. Although in the veteran stage, he was still a good player and he helped me a lot on the field. In fact both Blan brothers – Albert played for Swinton – were great players.

I certainly enjoyed my debut and felt that I had made a good impression generally. We won 12–4 and I came through unscathed, but things were about to change in that respect. When I played my second game I got an elbow in the mouth that dislodged my front teeth. It was against Belle Vue Rangers. A few weeks later the surgeon, who had his surgery at Prescot Road, said he would have to take them out, because they were too badly damaged. It was quite deliberate. I was tackling someone and he led with his forearm. Don't forget in those days that since there were no substitutes, it was a real advantage to get your opposite number off the pitch. It was a fact of life in the game then.

I never heard coaches say directly that they wanted opposition players taken out of the game, but Vinty [Vince Karalius] could build himself up for the game by focussing on a particular individual. "I'm going to get that bastard today," he would say to me. "If you can find him from the kick-off, I'll have him." Like today's kickers, I used to place the ball so that it inclined towards me. When I kicked it, the ball would go quite high and spin backwards. The poor bugger on Vinty's 'hit-list' would catch it and take the full force of a crunching tackle.

In fact, because I had my front teeth knocked out, I used to get a lot of internal cuts inside the mouth. My 'eye' teeth were a bit of a problem and when I got hit, they would cut my mouth on the inside. Saints made me a gumshield, but I couldn't wear it. I found that I couldn't breathe properly. Ironically, I wear a gumshield now despite having retired from competitive rugby many years ago. My dentist told me that I must grind my teeth when I'm asleep, so he made me a gumshield to minimise the damage.

The final match of the season at Barrow was a bit of a disappointment as we slumped to a 26–3 defeat. It was Abe Terry's debut in the front row that day, although he won't thank me for mentioning it. As for me, I had made the transition into the first team successfully and looked forward to more of the same in 1955–56. Our coach Jim Sullivan certainly seemed to have confidence in my ability. He had played in the same era as Billy Mercer and was the club's first full-time coach and his word was law – very much like Sir Alex Ferguson in football. He dominated everything at the club. Fortunately, he seemed to think the world of me and treated me accordingly. I remember when he became very ill in the early 1970s and I went to visit him in hospital in Wigan. He had previously had a stroke and was not in good shape at all. He recognised me straightaway and called me by name. His wife was pleasantly surprised that he had made the connection. Apparently he had not spoken for quite some time. She thanked me for my visit and I believe he passed away shortly afterwards. A real shame – he was such a great man and a huge figure in rugby league.

It wasn't just in rugby terms that my life changed when I left school in 1952. At the age of 16 I signed apprenticeship forms with Ashdown's, a subsidiary of Pilkington Brothers, based near to Saints' ground in Eccleston. Duggie Greenall worked there as a fitter, although in a different workshop to me. My apprenticeship as a toolmaker lasted for five years.

Learning my trade as an apprentice toolmaker at Ashdown's.

The former Ashdown's factory (then called Triplex) was demolished in 2008.

By the time it finished, I had been transferred to Pilkington's Ravenhead works, when Ashdown's closed, just before my National Service came along. One of my first tasks was to make templates for the manufacture of television screens. The templates would be made according to the draughtsman's specifications. Once the mould had been made they would go to the press, where a plunger would turn the molten glass into the final product. We also made glass for car doors and, at one time, we were involved in making night-time camera lenses for the SAS for use in the jungle. It was highly-specialised stuff where measurements would come down to a thousandth of an inch.

It was important to learn a trade, but there were occasions when I was not able to work half-days because of rugby commitments. I had one particular foreman, who was, shall we say, a bit awkward when it came to getting time off. I remember one occasion when we were due to play in Cumbria and there was no way I could turn in on Saturday morning, because the team coach would leave at eight o'clock. I duly made my request to this fellow and he played hell. "You are getting paid to be an apprentice toolmaker." He went on and on with his tirade – in front of the lads too.

I was just turned 18 or something like that and the way I had been treated genuinely upset me. I later phoned the Saints' secretary, Basil Lowe, and he said he would see what he could do. Basil went right to the top. He contacted Sir Harry Pilkington, no less, who sent one of the big bosses down to the factory, ending with the foreman getting a good talking to. He went as white as a sheet when he realised what was going to happen and I think he was expecting to be sacked. Sir Harry [later Lord] Pilkington was a Saints diehard and obviously had the needs of the club at heart. Apart from his objectionable manner, I do think that my foreman was perhaps a little envious of me with my rugby career taking off at Knowsley Road, but it didn't happen again and I was able to have the best of both worlds in a way. It was also good publicity for the firm to have a successful rugby league player on the workforce.

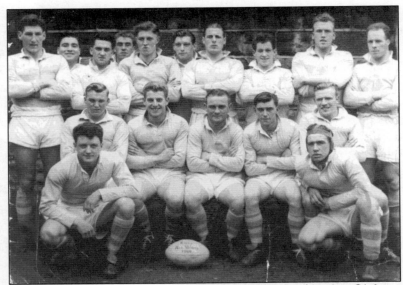

St Helens 'A' 69 Blackpool Borough 'A' 7. Lancashire Combination, 21 August 1954 at Knowsley Road. Back: Vince Karalius, Cliff Johnson, Frank McCabe, Eric Ledger, J. Spencer, Bill Boycott, Roy Robinson, Billy Adams, Josh Gaskell, J. Booth; front: Arthur Pimblett, Alec Davies, Joe Ball, Tommy Finn, T. Lomas; kneeling: Austin Rhodes, Len McIntyre.

An early outing in the Saints' first team. St Helens 17 Barrow 31. Ward Cup, 13 April 1955 at Knowsley Road. Attendance: 8,000. Back: Duggie Greenall, Austin Rhodes, Frank Carlton, Alec Davies, Glyn Moses, Bill Finnan, Brian Howard; front: Billy Blan, Pat Lannon, Josh Gaskell, Alan Prescott (c), Bill Bretherton, George Parsons.

4. All the way to Wembley

"In 1956 I was doing my National Service but managed to get to Wembley to watch the Saints play Halifax. The scrum-half that day was Austin Rhodes, who I knew about from his days with – rather fittingly – St Austin's School in Thatto Heath. He was a great schoolboy star, a talented footballer and he became a great goalkicker. Austin was someone to be reckoned with on the field and could hold his own in any company. He had a great game at Wembley, with his half-back partner Bill Finnan. Hard to believe he was the 'babe' of the team aged just 19."

Denis Whittle
Saints supporter and local journalist

The 1955–56 season was my first full one in the first team. I felt really strong and fit, and was quite confident in my own ability as a rugby league player. Jim Sullivan was still at the helm, which was another reason why I was upbeat about the future season. He always rated me as a player. When I got into the first team initially, it was at stand-off; in 1955–56, I played at scrum-half in virtually every match. I was a member of the 'second phase' of Jim Sullivan's team-building at Saints, with several new faces coming into the side from when he first arrived in 1952, such as Nat Silcock and Frank Carlton, who made 38 appearances and scored 40 tries that season. Vince Karalius was also by now an established member of the team. There was still the core of Sully's original team, including Duggie Greenall, Steve Llewellyn, Glyn Moses, George Parsons and our skipper, Alan Prescott. Little wonder we finished in the top four and broke our duck in the Challenge Cup.

As it turned out, the 1955–56 season gave me an extra responsibility within the team – something that I could have lived without really – goalkicking. Goalkicking was thrust upon me. I had never really kicked a rugby ball, but I was always a fair footballer and it was never too much trouble to boot a few over. When I played as a schoolboy, there was a lad called Jimmy Swift who played in the centre for our school and for Lancashire Schoolboys, and he was a phenomenal kicker. Consequently I never needed to kick goals. I used to practice occasionally on the Vine Tavern pitches, but not really seriously. It was in our match against York at Knowsley Road in our fourth game of the season, when I first put boot to ball. It was a sad match for our normal kicker, Peter Metcalfe, another former St Austin's lad like me, who was carried off with a serious knee injury which ended his career. We hadn't been playing all that long and I gave Peter a simple ball from the scrum base. Peter took it on the run – a little wide – and I think he intended giving the ball to the inside centre and float round for a pass. He was good at this and used to make a lot of breaks this way. The opposing stand-off just tackled him as he passed the ball. It was an innocuous tackle, but he ended up with a cracked kneecap and never put a pair of boots on again. We had scored a few tries, had a few penalties and various people had tried to kick for goal, including Duggie Greenall and George Parsons, without success – and that was putting it mildly.

In the end, Alan Prescott was looking round to see if anyone else would have a go. I just thought it was a ridiculous situation so I asked for the ball. I ended up kicking four out of four that day and Jim Sullivan was delighted. He'd found a kicker he didn't know he had, purely by accident. I kicked all the way through then. I kicked with 'soft toes' and didn't use any special boots like some players did. I never professed to be a goalkicker and I was always happy if anyone else wanted to have a go and thought they could do a better job. In fact, after the York match I had a bit of a purple patch with the boot, with eight in the next game, 12 against Barrow and seven against Blackpool Borough. All the games were at Knowsley Road. I finished the season with 138 goals and 10 tries for a total of 306 points, so I had made a worthwhile contribution to the team.

Blazing a trail in the Challenge Cup

The team continued to do well as the season went on. We won 20–6 at Leigh on 2 January in front of over 16,000 fans, and I kicked another 12 goals a week later when we beat Salford 48–2 at Knowsley Road. It was the Challenge Cup in the New Year too and we began our cup campaign at home with a 15–6 victory against Warrington with 23,000 in attendance. I can remember having to mark their danger man Gerry Helme, who formed a great combination with Ray Price, who later came to Knowsley Road. The match was only saved from being postponed because of the braziers used to keep the ice off the pitch, but there were still some areas where the pitch was very hard indeed. I can remember Abe Terry picking up one of their forwards and dumping him onto the turf. He banged his head and had to go off. If it was where one of the braziers had been, he would have been as fit as a fiddle.

The luck of the draw gave us another home tie against Castleford, who were not a great side by any means and we won 48–5 without too much trouble. We were at home again in round three, which paired us with Bradford Northern, who had been the Saints' bogey team in the late 1940s and early 1950s in the cup. Saints had played them six times and had not managed to score a try against them. Bradford Northern were not quite the team they had been, however and we produced a fantastic performance to beat them 53–6, with Frank Carlton racing in for four tries. I kicked 10 goals and followed it up a week later with seven when we battered Wigan 29–7 on Good Friday, in front of 32,000 packed into Knowsley Road.

Unfortunately our hooker Frank McCabe, a Thatto Heath lad and a great friend of mine, picked up a severe knee injury against Bradford that ended his career. Frank was a great player, who scored two tries in that match. He was replaced by Len McIntyre, another fine hooker with a good pair of hands, but it was so unlucky for Frank to pick up his injury when he did – a cruel blow indeed.

We were firing on all cylinders, but the best was still to come, when we were drawn against Barrow in the semi-final of the Challenge Cup. It took two matches to dispose of them and they were both brilliant games. The first was on the Saturday at Swinton and ended 5–5, Frank Carlton scored Saints' try, and the second was on the following Tuesday at Wigan, in front of over 44,000 spectators. There were thousands locked out or those who just couldn't get to the ground in time. The replay was 0–0 after normal time. I find it amusing when people today talk about fabulous games with 60 or more points being scored. For me, this scoreless draw was one the best games I have played in. Todder Dickinson was my half-back partner and I marked a fellow called Dick Harris. Willie Horne was the stand-off, a great player and a gentleman. He had a good tactical head on his shoulders, and a great pair of hands, although he didn't have much pace to speak of. He took the goalkicks too. I remember they could have beaten us in the dying seconds of the first match, when they were awarded a penalty, but he didn't have the power. Ironically, if Joe Ball, the former Saints star had been playing, he might have had the power to boot it over the sticks, but Horne's effort fell short and we lived to play again. The replay was famous for Steve Llewellyn's famous long-distance try when he handed off his opposite number, Frank Castle, twice before diving over the line. It was a great try – probably the best of Steve's career, but not quite as good as van Vollenhoven's against Hunslet in 1959, which is the best I've ever seen. George Parsons scored the other try for us and we were on our way to Wembley after our 10–5 success. The semi-final replay was fantastic, though – the tension, the excitement and the massive crowd, plus 0–0 at the end of normal time all added to the great rugby played by the two sides. Some great scrambling defence too.

Battle of the Roses

So we were going to Wembley, which was such an unbelievable thrill for a youngster like me. The squad stayed in Southport. We changed at the Queen's Hotel on the front which had its own swimming pool. We then went by coach to the King George V Playing Fields, where we trained, from Monday to Wednesday of Cup Final week. They did say later that the turf on those pitches was very similar to what we could expect at Wembley, but I didn't think it made too much difference for us. After training we went back to the hotel, had five minutes in the pool and showered, before having a meal. One evening I went to have a walk around the fairground with Vinty and we ended up going to see a gypsy fortune teller. Vinty was very superstitious. She says: "I can see you both holding a trophy up. Are you sportsmen? What do you play? Snooker? Crown green bowls?" Vinty genuinely believed that it was all over and Halifax would have no chance. "That's it Austin," he said. "It's the Challenge Cup she's talking about." For all we knew the clairvoyant might well have been a Saints fan, but it certainly did wonders for Vinty's morale.

On Thursday we went to our headquarters at Richmond, near Old Deer Park Surrey. Amazingly, on the Saturday morning, I went for a stroll with Vinty and Jack Wilkinson and Stan Kielty of Halifax were coming towards us. I acknowledged Kielty "Are you all right?" Vinty got a bit mad with me as a result. "What are you talking to him for?" He then shouted to Kielty: "If you come round the blind side this afternoon I'll pick you up with my finger and thumb and throw you into the crowd." I thought that if we weren't careful, we'd be fighting before we started. Vinty was a great friend of mine at the time and this was his way of asserting himself and getting a psychological advantage.

The week before Wembley, we had a 'dress rehearsal' against the same opponents at Thrum Hall in the Championship semi-final. As the third-placed team in the league, we played the team in second place, away, who just happened to be Halifax. We lost 23–8 – Halifax eventually lost in the Championship Final to Hull – and Todder Dickinson received the knee injury which not only ruled him out of Wembley seven days later, but also dogged him for the rest of his career. If he had received the injury today, perhaps the prognosis would not have been so bad. John had been my partner at stand-off for much of the season and Bill Finnan came in for him for the final.

I remember talking to Nat Silcock after the game at Thrum Hall and he told me not to worry unduly about the result too much. "I'll tell you this, Austin," he said. "They won't be able to handle me at Wembley. They won't know which way I'm going to go." He was very confident about that and, of course, he was proved to be quite correct. Nat was a big fellow, with tremendous pace and a terrific 'ramrod' hand-off. He was also a great bloke to have to lift team spirits. I don't think he got the credit he deserved. Nat was almost as good as Dick Huddart.

There was another headache for Jim Sullivan and his team selection, an injury to Walter Delves in the back-row. It was down to two players – Josh Gaskell and Roy Robinson. When Sully announced his team, with Roy Robinson in the second-row, Josh was quite naturally very upset. I would have put Josh in the side, personally, simply because he had more size and power than Roy and was pretty mobile too. Neither Robinson nor Gaskell had played in any of the previous rounds of the competition. For all that, the coach had chosen a team that went on to lift the trophy, so he was vindicated.

We had breakfast at the hotel and then had our infamous stroll around the grounds, where we met some of our future opponents. Afterwards, we got our gear ready for the relatively short coach ride to Wembley. The stadium was magical, with great facilities. I saw all the communal baths – it was quite a contrast to a couple of washbasins when I started playing at school. Everything was laid on for us.

Have a drink on us, Precky. Skipper Alan Prescott drinks from the Challenge Cup in the Wembley dressing room. Back: Steve Llewellyn, Duggie Greenall, George Parsons; front: Glyn Moses, Brian Howard, Frank Carlton, Bill Finnan, Jim Sullivan (coach), Nat Silcock, Alan Prescott (c), Len McIntyre, Vince Karalius, Roy Robinson, Austin Rhodes.

This lad Rhodes will be a belter. The Wembley return and I am introduced to the crowd in the Town Hall Square by chairman Harry Cook. When Duggie Greenall came on, he did his usual rendition of *Mammy*.

As for the match, there were shades of the semi-final when for a long time it was total stalemate, until Frank Carlton scored in the 66th minute. Before that, we had a really good chance of breaking the deadlock when Alan Prescott made a break on the left-hand side of the pitch, from our own 25 yard line. Unfortunately, he had Frank Carlton on the wing virtually unopposed, but his pass failed and the chance was gone. I was practising the goalkick in my head and the next minute, we were scrumming down. Although he was captain of club, county and country at the time, he wasn't a great passer. Alan did score the last try to secure the victory, however. As for kicking at Wembley, people used to say that the wind would swirl around and do things to the ball, but it didn't seem to deviate too much. I found that if I kicked the ball cleanly and true, there was no real problem, although nerves did play a big part in such a big match. I was as nervous as anyone else.

Alan Prescott was chosen as the Lance Todd Trophy winner, and in the end we won 13–2 in front of just under 80,000 fans.

St Helens (0) 13 Halifax (0) 2
Challenge Cup Final
28 April 1956 at Wembley Stadium
Attendance: 79,341
St Helens: Glyn Moses, Steve Llewellyn, Duggie Greenall, Brian Howard, Frank Carlton, Bill Finnan, Austin Rhodes, Alan Prescott (c), Len McIntyre, Nat Silcock, George Parsons, Roy Robinson, Vince Karalius.
Scorers: Tries: Llewellyn, Prescott, Carlton. Goals: Rhodes (2).
Halifax: Tus Griffiths, Arthur Daniels, Tommy Lynch, Geoff Palmer, Johnnie Freeman, Ken Dean, Stan Kielty, Jack Wilkinson, Alvin Ackerley (c), John Henderson, Albert Fearnley, Les Pearce, Ken Traill.
Scorer: Goal: Griffiths.
Referee: Ron Gelder (Wakefield)
Lance Todd Trophy winner: Alan Prescott (St Helens)

After the match and the celebrations on the pitch and in the spacious dressing room, we went down to the Metropole Hotel in Brighton for the rest of the weekend. The hotel was next door to the Grand Hotel which was targeted by the IRA in 1984 when the Conservative Party Conference was in town. We had our photograph taken outside the front of the hotel with our supporters who had come down with us –

another memorable moment. We then got a coach back to London and went back to Liverpool on the train from Euston.

There was an open-topped bus waiting for us at Lime Street to take us back to St Helens. I couldn't believe the reception we got from people in Liverpool as we headed back home. We returned to an absolutely packed Town Hall Square where we showed the cup to the supporters. Chairman Harry Cook introduced each one of us to the crowd. We all had to say a few words, but he didn't get too much out of me. Alan Prescott gave a speech, but Steve Llewellyn surprised me a bit. I expected him to say much more than he did, seeing he was a schoolteacher by profession, but the occasion could have got to anyone. He just waved, in the end.

Duggie gave us a rousing rendition of his theme song *Mammy* and compared to 1953, this time he was in front of so many people as a winner. I have many happy memories of Duggie and we became great friends. It was always a great atmosphere when we used to return home from matches on the coach and Duggie used to sing brilliantly to entertain us. I'm sure he could have earned a living doing it. Vinty used to fancy his chances as a singer too, but he wasn't quite in the same league as Duggie. His voice was more like a foghorn. Yet both were wonderful company and great blokes to have on your side.

Overall, things could not have gone any better for both me and the team. Winning at Wembley – and for the first time in the club's history – was the ultimate. We had great spectators cheering us on all the way and they were fantastic times. We hoped to maintain our success as a team and retain the Challenge Cup in 1956–57. On a personal note, I hoped to continue my progress and hope that I might be given a chance at representative level.

Hail the Challenge Cup winners. Back: Duggie Greenall, Roy Robinson, Nat Silcock, Steve Llewellyn, Vince Karalius, George Parsons, Abe Terry (reserve), Reg Senior (reserve); front: Len McIntyre, Bill Finnan, Austin Rhodes, Alan Prescott (c), Jim Sullivan (coach), Glyn Moses, Frank Carlton, John Dickinson (reserve), Brian Howard.

No hard feelings. Having a drink with former Halifax stand-off Ken Dean at the Saints' Past Players' Dinner in 2008 – 52 years after our Wembley success.

Getting in some kicking practice at Knowsley Road.

5. A bitter-sweet experience

"From day one I thought this lad was one who was going to be a big success in rugby league. The thing is, he was such a good all-round footballer. Austin began as a stand-off, of course but he could also play centre and scrum half and kick goals as well. He eventually took over the full-back position from me when I retired through injury and did a cracking job. I thought he had a bit more room to move in that position. But he would be in my team any time. He could also look after himself on the field. Believe me, nobody took advantage of him. If they did, he could 'stick one on' his opponent, as the saying goes. He was hard as nails. We toured in 1957 and being among the 'big boys' did him a power of good and really brought his game on."
Glyn Moses
St Helens RLFC 1953 to 1960

At the end of the 1955–56 season, the club had won the Challenge Cup for the first time in its history and provided me with my first winner's medal. I felt as though I was there to stay in the first team and that we had a good chance of gaining further honours. Unfortunately this was not the case in 1956–57. On a personal note, only Nat Silcock, with 42 appearances, played more matches than I did and I finished up with 25 tries and 145 goals from 41 games.

We were the highest scoring and best defensive team in the league and yet didn't win any cups. In the first round of the Lancashire Cup we beat Swinton; Liverpool City in the second and then beat Warrington at Wilderspool 17–9 in front of 26,000 in the semi-final. There were 40,000 at the final at Central Park, Wigan, to see us lose 10–3 to a great Oldham side. Memories of this match are a bit hazy – I must only remember the games we won – but Josh Gaskell played in the second-row with George Parsons, and Vinty played loose-forward. I was at stand-off, with John 'Todder' Dickinson at scrum-half. We didn't really have enough possession from the scrums to make an impact.

Someone also told me that Oldham kept the ball for 42 tackles at one stage – no wonder we couldn't get a look in. Possession was the law in those days. On the Oldham side, they had the likes of Frank Pitchford, Sid Little and Derek Turner – really great players. Derek

Turner scored the only points of the second half with the try that sealed victory for them with just a couple of minutes to go. They went on to win the Championship and Lancashire League at the end of the season and it was a pity that such a team never went on to lift the Challenge Cup at Wembley, or even play at the famous stadium for that matter. Saints finished in fifth place in the league at the end of the season and did not qualify for the top four play-offs.

Oldham (7) 10 St Helens (3) 3
Lancashire Cup Final
20 October 1956 at Central Park, Wigan
Attendance: 39,544
Over 39,000 fans saw the Roughyeds from Oldham come through victorious in a real 'bash-and-batter' affair in the mud at Central Park. This was a match won by the Oldham forwards in a tremendous second-half spell when they showed true grit and determination. At one stage they were able to hold the ball for 34 tackles before being dispossessed. The St Helens threequarters were generally starved of quality possession, although winger Frank Carlton gave them hope with a sparkling individual effort. A try by John Etty plus two goals from Bernard Ganley gave Oldham a 7–3 advantage at half-time. Oldham scored a try right on the final whistle, courtesy of loose-forward 'Rocky' Turner. But Saints had been tackled out of it by then.
Oldham: Bernard Ganley, Dick Cracknell, Denis Ayres, Alan Davies, John Etty, Frank Stirrup, Frank Pitchford, Ken Jackson, Dick Keith, Don Vines, Sid Little, Charlie Winslade, Derek Turner.
Scorers: Tries: Etty, Turner. Goals: Ganley 2.
St Helens: Glyn Moses, Steve Llewellyn, Duggie Greenall, Bill Finnan, Frank Carlton, John Dickinson, Austin Rhodes, Alan Prescott (c), Len McIntyre, Nat Silcock, George Parsons, Josh Gaskell, Vince Karalius.
Scorer: Try: Carlton.
Referee: Matt Coates (Pudsey)

In the autumn of 1956 there were rumours in the newspapers and among the supporters that Saints were going to sign Cliff Morgan, the Welsh rugby union international fly-half. It was no rumour – I met him at Knowsley Road during a training session and we shook hands. I think he had been inside the ground with Jim Sullivan to have a look at the pitch and he was then brought out to have a word with some of the players. I don't know why he did not sign for St Helens in the end – perhaps living up north did not appeal to him – but he was a great player who would have been a huge success in rugby league. We never saw him again after that. There must have been a strong interest in changing codes on his part to have come up in the first place. As for my own situation, at some stage I was going to do my National Service and therefore the club would need another stand-off at some point.

In November, we played against the Australian tourists at Knowsley Road in one of the most incredible matches I have ever taken part in.

The *St Helens Reporter* had the headline: "Saints good enough to be selected for Great Britain en bloc." The match report went on to say: "Aided by a good service from the scrums, John Dickinson and Austin Rhodes were in rare form at half-back. They never dominated the play because both preferred to act as links rather than finishers of movements. Both scored, but it was in their general approach play and intelligent work in the loose that they shone."

We retained our record as the only side undefeated by the Australians up to then in post-war matches. The pack at that time was especially mobile and the players were more than capable of scoring tries. I marked Keith Holman, who had quite a reputation in the green and gold jersey as a class player – and a tough bugger too. I think I handled the threat from my opposite number reasonably well, given the score.

St Helens (3) 44 Australia (0) 2
Tour Match
24 November 1956 at Knowsley Road, St Helens
Attendance: 17,100
St Helens: Glyn Moses, Steve Llewellyn, Duggie Greenall, Bill Finnan,
Frank Carlton, John Dickinson, Austin Rhodes, Alan Prescott (c), Frank McCabe,
Abe Terry, Nat Silcock, Josh Gaskell, Vince Karalius.
Scorers: Tries: Llewellyn 2, Dickinson, Rhodes, Prescott, McCabe, Terry,
Silcock, Gaskell, Karalius. Goals: Rhodes 7.
Australia: Gordon Clifford, Denis Flannery, Alex Watson, Dick Poole,
Don Adams, Bobby Banks, Keith Holman, Brian Davies, Ken Kearney, Roy Bull,
Bill Marsh, Don Furner, Bill Tyquin.
Scorer: Goal: Clifford.
Referee: Mr Smith (Barrow)

It was not unreasonable to say that we were favourites to retain the Challenge Cup when the competition started in the new year. We were drawn away to Whitehaven – not the easiest of places to go. I played scrum-half that day and it was soon obvious that the home team would do anything to gain an advantage. As soon as the first scrum went down, one of the Whitehaven second-rowers smashed our hooker Tom McKinney's nose all over his face. Tom retaliated and got sent off so we were left with 12 men for the remaining 75 minutes. They were all laughing their heads off — I don't think they could believe their luck. Obviously we lost the match because we could not get any ball from the scrums. Possession was everything in those days.

	P	W	D	L	F	A	Pts
Oldham	38	33	0	5	893	365	66
Hull	38	29	2	7	764	432	60
Barrow	38	29	0	9	702	481	58
Leeds	38	28	0	10	818	490	56
St Helens	38	25	3	10	902	355	53
Wigan	38	26	0	12	750	417	52
Hunslet	38	26	0	12	688	417	52
Wakefield Trinity	38	23	1	14	747	545	47

The top eight clubs in 1956–57; St Helens were just outside the play-off places.

Although the domestic season had proved disappointing in terms of not winning a major trophy — something the team was more than capable of — I was selected for the World Cup squad to go to Australia at the end of the season. I had already been a reserve for the Great Britain versus France match at Knowsley Road, so my name must have been in the frame. I was the youngest player selected and it was a tremendous honour to be in the squad. Great Britain were the holders of the World Cup, having won it in 1954 as underdogs. We had just beaten the Australians in the home test match series and were expected to do well.

Unfortunately, I had this feeling that I wasn't going to be strong enough for the hurly-burly of test matches in Australia. So I started weightlifting at an old place near Toll Bar Congs — with a fellow named Jack Bradbury. He had what you would call 'muscles on muscles.' We did some weightlifting and I developed a problem with my back. I suppose I was a bit stupid to do the extra weights in the first place and the injury soon began to take its toll. My form dipped and I really didn't deserve my place in the squad at one stage. Basil Lowe, the club secretary, ended up sending me to a guy called Neil Johnson in Rodney

Street, Liverpool, who was a qualified osteopath. He said that I had a trapped nerve and an appending disc problem. He manipulated me a couple of times and I'll never forget the feeling. Jim Sullivan even had to strap my back up a certain way before a match. He had to stick layers of plaster across my lower back that eventually would prevent the disk from bulging any further. Fortunately things gradually started to improve and I can remember having a blinder against Jeff Stevenson at Leeds and I felt so much better – quicker and stronger. Despite the improvement, I do believe that this injury has caused a lot of the problems I have experienced in later years with my hip. If someone's body is not aligned and they are compensating by putting pressure more on one side, then it can cause problems with their hips.

Despite the injury, I still went on the tour, although the first choice half-backs were Jeff Stevenson and Ray Price. I realised that perhaps my opportunities might be limited, because I was the only un-capped player. Another competitor for a half-back place was Lewis Jones, the 'Golden Boy' of rugby league. Three of my club team-mates also made the trip: skipper Alan Prescott, hooker Tom McKinney and full-back Glyn Moses.

Just getting to Australia was an exhausting experience. The flight was horrendous. We went from Manchester via London, Rome, Karachi, Calcutta, Singapore, Jakarta and finally arrived in Perth, three days later – where it was 90 degrees. We stayed in a fabulous hotel. I roomed with Glyn Moses wherever we went on tour. On the first morning in the hotel in Australia I went down for breakfast dressed casually and Bill Fallowfield, the RFL general secretary and tour manager, looked me up-and-down and said "If I ever see you dressed like that again you will be on the first flight home. You are representing your country, never forget that." Fallowfield was the top man – he organised everything and his word was the law. To be fair, I didn't take my ball home. Why should I?

While in Perth, we trained with the Western Australian Aussie Rules team and after a week it was on to Sydney to play for the World Cup, but not before a practice match against a Western Australian XIII, which we won 66–5. Unfortunately, this match was very costly for us with stand-off Ray Price injured and eventually sent home. Lewis Jones took his place and we won our opening game against France 23–5 at the Sydney Cricket Ground. The second match, against Australia was a disaster. Quite a few members of the team were carrying injuries and Australia beat us 31–6. The Australians could not be overhauled in the league table and were World Champions. It's well documented that Lewis Jones didn't have the best of games against Australia that day. Bill Fallowfield told him at the end of the match that he would never tour for Great Britain again. Lewis played at centre in the next match, which was good for me, however, and paved the way for me to make my international debut against New Zealand, at the Sydney Cricket Ground, in our last match of the tournament. The record books say that there was a crowd of just over 14,000 and our performance was quite disappointing too. We lost 29–21. I was concussed and had eight stitches in my mouth on my debut. At least I had played a part, but it was not what I would have really wanted.

New Zealand 29 Great Britain 21
World Cup Match
25 June 1957 at Sydney Cricket Ground
Referee: Darcy Lawler (Australia)
New Zealand: Pat Creedy, Bernard Hadfield, Bill Sorenson, George Turner, Reece Griffiths, George Menzies, Sel Belsham, Bill McLennan, Jock Butterfield, John Yates, Henry Maxwell, Cliff Johnson (c), Jim Riddell.
Scorers: Tries: Hadfield, Turner, Menzies, McLennan. Goals: Sorensen 7.
Great Britain: Glyn Moses, Eric Ashton, Phil Jackson, Lewis Jones, Mick Sullivan, Austin Rhodes, Jeff Stevenson; Alan Prescott (c), Tom McKinney, Sid Little, Jack Grundy, Geoff Gunney, Derek Turner.
Scorers: Tries: Jackson, Jones, Sullivan, Little, Grundy. Goals: Jones 3.
Attendance: 14,263

Despite our disappointment at not retaining the World Cup, there was more rugby and travelling for the squad before we got back to Blighty – quite an experience for a youngster like me and I played in every match from then on. From Sydney we went to Brisbane and played Queensland where we won comfortably 44–5. We then flew to Auckland and played another match against a French XIII, which we won 26–12, before some sightseeing, including the springs at Rotorua. Alan Prescott got badly hurt against France in the World Cup match and when we arrived at our New Zealand hotel he collapsed with delayed concussion. He was in hospital for a week after that.

Even then, there was more to come. We flew back to Sydney and then across the Indian Ocean to Mauritius, before landing in

Johannesburg. We played the French in a series of matches in South Africa. They were meant to be exhibition matches to promote rugby league there, but became quite violent affairs and they didn't seem to like us that much. It was to try and get the game going over there. Mind you, we had to leave Billy Boston behind because of apartheid. This really upset the lads, as he was a really popular member of the team. We played at Benoni, Durban and East London, before flying home from Johannesburg to Manchester at the end of July.

Was the visit to South Africa worthwhile? Shortly after it, Saints signed the greatest player ever to play rugby league in my opinion – Tom van Vollenhoven. Apart from the injury against New Zealand I loved everything about the trip and all the hotels were superb. I was just 20 years old and had already played in some of the great rugby stadiums of the world. A great shame we couldn't retain the World Cup, but our time, and mine, was to come in 1960.

The 1957 World Cup does have an enduring legacy for my family, which lasts to this day. When I first stayed in Perth I fell in love with the place. When my daughter Karen decided to migrate to Australia in the late 1980s I persuaded her to settle down in Perth and we visit her whenever we can. It is the perfect antidote to these increasingly harsh English winters. Karen became an Australian citizen in June 2010 and in the ceremony wore an Australian international jersey I swapped with Keith Barnes after a World Cup clash in 1960, when we won the competition.

St Helens (3) 16 Oldham (13) 25, league match, 8 September 1956 at Knowsley Road. Attendance: 26,000. I was in great fettle then and am going for the gap as Vince Karalius (left) is bottled up by Oldham's John Etty. Derek 'Rocky' Turner (in scrum-cap) is lurking menacingly.

Great Britain 29 France 14. Test match 10 April 1957. The Great Britain team, plus reserves, on the training pitch at Knowsley Road before the game, which drew a 20,928 crowd.

Left: Enjoying Neilson Beach in Sydney with Mick Sullivan during the 1957
World Cup. In his pomp he was the best left winger I've ever seen.
Right: Billy Boston enjoys the sights in the Blue Mountains.

A proud moment – lining up for my portrait as a member of the Great Britain
World Cup squad in 1957. (Courtesy Robert Gate)

I am on the far right of this picture, next to Eric Ashton, at Durban beach towards the end of the World Cup tour in 1957. We were both planning to send 'contractual' letters to our respective clubs when we got back to England.

Strewth! Our daughter, Karen, became an Australian citizen in 2007 and during the ceremony, she wore the Australian jersey I swapped with Keith Barnes after the 1960 World Cup. (Courtesy Karen Rhodes)

6. Your country needs you

"Austin and I played in the 1956 Challenge Cup Final although we had another distinction in that we both represented the RAF at rugby union when we did our National Service. He went in after me, but he was such a good all-round player he would have excelled at either code. I was a Leading Aircraftsman and like Austin and Alex Murphy a few years later, based at Haydock, although I lived at home in Clinkham Wood. I remember that they were looking for Welsh lads at first to trial for rugby, but when they knew I had played for Saints they gave me a go. I played for my Command and then went into the full RAF team. I introduced our coach at Saints, Jim Sullivan, to Wing Commander Cameron, who was the secretary of RAF rugby. When I got into the RAF team, they would ask me if there were any other lads from the professional ranks who were going to follow me and I would tell them."
Brian Howard
St Helens RLFC 1952 to 1959

It all started after the 1956 Challenge Cup Final. In the dressing room Jim Sullivan introduced both Frank Carlton and I to a guy named Wing Commander Cameron. We shook hands and he said that when National Service time arrived, after we had done our apprenticeships, he wanted us to join the RAF and they would look after us and maybe get us posted closer to home. I had two years to wait, but Frank Carlton was two years older than me so he went in virtually straight away. The age to start National Service in those days was 18, but if someone had an apprenticeship, they had to finish that first and would go in at 21. In my case at the age of 21 I was a fully qualified toolmaker; Frank Carlton was a fully qualified gas fitter.

As for Wing Commander Cameron coming into our dressing room, that was typical of Jim Sullivan. He was a great bloke and a fantastic coach, but was certainly a bit of a wheeler-dealer. He seemed to have connections everywhere. National Service posed a bit of a threat to team-building when a coach or chairman knew that a player could, possibly, be missing for two years and the clubs had to make plans.

I got my call up papers in February 1958 and caught a train from Liverpool Lime Street to Bridgnorth, in Shropshire, to begin my eight weeks of basic training, ready to serve Queen and country for the next two years. I arrived at the camp and was left in no doubt as soon as I got there that it was going to be a rough time. The Sergeant in charge of us immediately picked on me. He bawled and shouted about my attitude and he made it quite clear he was going to give me a hard time, which he certainly did for the first two weeks. All the officers at the camp were all really keen on sport, however and there was a very intense rivalry between the squadrons. Perhaps there was an opportunity to become involved in sport that would help to alleviate the misery of daily chores.

Boxing clever

The rugby season had not started, so when someone asked whether anyone could box, I put my hand up straight away. I was brought up in a boxing environment. My father did a bit of professional boxing and my uncle Billy taught boxing at a gym in Prescot and had a few professionals boxing for him. My dad and I were fanatical about the sport at one stage, and followed Peter Kane, Randolph Turpin and Benny Lynch. We used to stay up for hours listening to boxing on the radio. At our house I used to have a punch bag and would spend up to an hour a day getting my timing right.

I was told to get down to the gym and the instructor thought that I had done quite a bit of boxing after watching me. He was surprised when I told him that I had never actually fought anyone despite being brought up in a keen boxing environment. The instructor then told me to get in the ring and have a bout with a bloke who supposedly had 53 fights – or so he said. I watched him training and honestly thought that it was all a bit of hype. He wasn't all that good in my opinion. In the end it was a bit of a mismatch, to say the least, and he got quite a battering. I was told I was going to fight for the Squadron and I would be excused all duties to train for the fight, which is exactly what I wanted. However, I knew that the rugby season would soon be starting and there was no chance that I would be allowed to box once they knew I was an international rugby player.

I remember one of the first training sessions we had for the rugby team. It was tick rugby and I had just scored a try under the sticks when this Welsh lad came over to me. "No, no boyo," he said. "When you come to the full-back and you have got someone there you lean over like this and that's how you do it." I suppose he was correct in a way, if you had an extra man, but the player I had in support couldn't keep up with me, so I just waltzed round the full-back and did my own thing. Just as the lecture on passing ended, a guy ran onto the field and asked who the 'British Lion' was. I put my hand up and my Welsh 'coach' was by now unbelievably embarrassed and could not get out of the way quickly enough. Incidentally, the Sergeant who had given me a rough time during my early days was by now polishing my boots for me and when our Squadron won the championship and I scored the winning try and kicked the goal, he positively adored me.

After finishing training and the dreaded 'square-bashing' at Bridgnorth, I was later sent down to Aylesbury in Buckinghamshire. I ended up playing for the RAF and I had a fabulous time as a result of my sporting connections. I spent quite a bit of time going to London. I would be given an order from the commanding officer with the full itinerary for a particular fixture, including train times, hotels, pre-match meal and tactical talk and we would go and play the game. Everything was laid on for us. We played all the top teams in the country with the RAF Rugby Union XV, such as Harlequins, who had two line-out forwards who were like giants to me. We played on all the famous grounds too, such as Cardiff Arms Park and Twickenham.

We had some great players in the team, starting with a fellow called Bernard Wright from Birkenhead Park at full-back; I was right centre to a brilliant winger called Bill Burgess, who went on to have a great career in rugby league. The other centre was a Welshman, Malcolm Price and our captain was Onllwyn Brace, the Welsh international scrum-half. We certainly were no mugs and we beat the Army and Navy to win the Services Championship for the first time for 39 years. The Army had always dominated the series.

I was lucky that my sport enabled me to have a slightly easier two years than most during National Service. For winning the Championship the RAF team was were invited to tour the continent and play a few teams in France and Italy. So there I was walking round the Coliseum in Rome and we ended up in Biarritz. Unfortunately, I couldn't play on tour, because of my professional connections, but they still took me with them. So I had played on all the best grounds in England and Wales and was banned from playing anywhere on the continent because I was a professional. Secretly, I was very pleased about that

47

ruling because I could drink a bit more than the other lads and did not need to worry about my fitness.

In Rome we were invited to an audience with the Pope. When I sent a letter home to my parents telling them about this possible meeting with His Holiness you can imagine they were very thrilled at the prospect. Sadly it was not to be – the audience was cancelled.

From Rome we flew to France for the game in Biarritz. After the match we all went out for a drink and because the flight home was very early next morning we decided to get a reasonably early night. On the walk home to the hotel we were shocked to find that we were all arrested by the gendarmes and put in jail on suspicion of being involved in a jewel robbery.

Although we were all fairly worse for wear with drink I thought that someone in our company would be able to speak French because they were all professional people, but I was wrong. We spent about two hours behind bars before someone came to us who spoke English and got us released just in time to pack our bags and get to the airport in time for the flight home. It was quite an eventful tour.

The home front

When I was in the RAF, the Saints could call on Ray Price, who had joined from Warrington, to fill in at stand-off. Although nearing the veteran stage, he was still a superb player. They also signed Peter Fearis in 1958–59, because they needed a kicker. I remember hitch-hiking back to watch the Lancashire Cup Final when they were beaten by Oldham and Fearis played as the goalkicking full-back. They also got defeated at Featherstone Rovers on two successive occasions in the Challenge Cup and I didn't play in either match. Once National Service had begun, a serviceman was at the beck-and-call of the Forces. If they said 'play in London next Saturday', that's where I went. I played some games on a weekend pass, but the problem was that I was not training with the lads and it was obviously more difficult to play.

For the first Featherstone cup tie I was doing my square-bashing at Bridgnorth and for the second match I was in Aylesbury. I got weekend passes and hitch-hiked north both times, even though I was not selected to play. There was no trouble in getting a lift in those days. As soon as the drivers saw the uniform, that was it. I went all over the

48

country in that way. I remember Duggie had a go at one of their spectators when the teams were going off. The players had to walk off through the crowd at Post Office Road. I was walking behind Duggie, in my RAF uniform and the next minute – boomph.

They went mad and the upshot was that we had a police escort to get back to the coach. They said that, but for the snow, they would have murdered us in the first match. They certainly did in the second. They were a good side, with a lad named Mullaney who ripped us to bits. Don Fox was at scrum-half, a great player too.

I was later stationed closer to home, at Wilmslow, where I passed my driving test. For the RAF matches I used to get my instructions to catch the train from there to Euston, where I would have bed and breakfast at a Services club and then on to the match. My sergeant at Wilmslow was Dai Rees, who was Ray Price's scrum-half at Belle Vue and he used to come over to Knowsley Road to watch some matches. He was a real rum lad. I would be in the Saints' dressing room half an hour before kick-off getting changed and this bloke would come in and say: "Austin, there's a Wing Commander Rees waiting for you." There he was all talking posh; he was a real bluffer, Dai.

"Austin, can you get me a ticket for the match?"

"Of course I can, Dai."

We received at least one complimentary ticket for matches anyhow.

Towards the end of my National Service I was stationed at Haydock. I could return to Thatto Heath for weekends. Joe Pickavance, who was a haulier and later a Saints director, knew the Station Commander at the camp and could get me released on occasions to play at Grange Park Golf Club, where I was a member. I was grateful for that.

I picked up a League Championship medal with the Saints while still in the Forces and it was obvious that there was a good relationship between my superiors at Haydock and the St Helens board. I really enjoyed my National Service days and because of my ability to play rugby at a high level, I was able to play in the same team as some fantastic players that I would not have had the opportunity to do without being called up. I made many friends and it was a happy time. Sport had enabled me to have a slightly easier two years than many and I certainly did not miss those dreaded chores around the barracks. I had the best of both worlds by playing both for the RAF and my professional club. For that I am eternally grateful.

Left: "Halt, who goes there?" Using a 303 rifle was an essential part of basic training at RAF Bridgnorth.

Top: Royal Air Force 11 Army 3, at Twickenham in early 1959. Back: Mr K. Kelleher (referee), AC LR Evans (Cardington), Fg Off FJS Walton (Gaydon), Flt Lt GJA Head (Brampton), Cpl RG Long (Innsworth), AC PE McGovern (Cardington), Fg Off JM Ross (Cosford), Sqn Ldr RV Stirling (touch judge); front: SAC RO Rawson (Wattisham), Fg Off PE Mettler (High Wycombe), Fg Off EJ Jones (Halton), Fg Off DO Brace (Captain - St Athan), Fg Off PW Watson (Benson), Plt Off BB Wright (Debden), AC W Burgess (Hereford); kneeling: SAC DW Phelps (Innsworth), AC AJ Rhodes (Wilmslow).

Right: I played for the RAF XV all over the country, including this game against Harlequins at the White City in London. My winger was my Saints' team-mate Frank Carlton. The referee was Denis Thatcher, husband of former Prime Minister Margaret Thatcher.

7. Champions and nearly men

"When I arrived at Saints, Austin had played in the World Cup in Australia the previous year. I didn't know that much about him, mind you, but I soon found out that above all else he was extremely cool under pressure; he was a great goalkicker and he would link up well in attack from the full-back position. Above all, he was a good reader of a game. Of all the games we played together, the 1961 Challenge Cup Final has got to be the highlight. It was the ultimate victory, especially because we were arguably the underdogs. We had some good nights out too. I worked at Lea Green Colliery as a fitter, so I tended to mate around with the Thatto Heath lads like Austin. Things were that much easier for me with lads like him. Plus, of course, there was Tommy Vol, Vince and Alex Murphy. They were great times with some fantastic memories."

Dick Huddart
St Helens RLFC 1958 to 1964

Like Alex Murphy, I was part of Jim Sullivan's second phase of team-building up at Knowsley Road. We were a good side, but still needed that something extra. During one training night, I realised that the club had made probably their greatest-ever signing. In the autumn of 1957 there were a lot of headlines about the Saints going after a South African rugby union winger called Tom van Vollenhoven. We were introduced to him by the coach, Jim Sullivan. We did some sprinting and he was like lightening. We then had a game of tick rugby and he scorched in for three or four tries in quick succession. I turned to Jim Sullivan and said: "Good God Jim, you've found us a jewel here." He couldn't stop laughing – just like someone who had won the pools.

Apparently the fans had been hankering for some new names at the time because they thought that our rugby was getting stale. The signing of Vol would have refreshed any team. He is the best player I've ever seen in my life. He had electrifying pace, a great hand-off and a fabulous body swerve. Brian Bevan was a fabulous player too, but he couldn't tackle as well as Tom. I got on great with Bevan. I thought he was a gentleman and obviously a fabulous player. If I had played for Warrington, perhaps I would have argued that he was the best player. But for me it was always 'Vol'. He was the complete player.

51

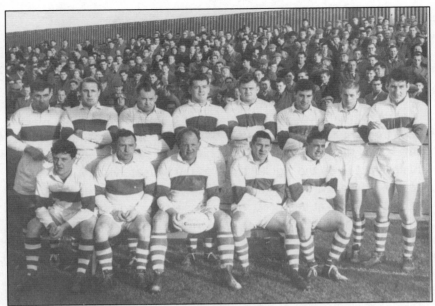

A happy Xmas. We hammered Wakefield at Knowsley Road and I scored four tries and kicked eight goals. Meanwhile, Tom van Vollenhoven scored six tries and equaled the club record. St. Helens 52 Wakefield Trinity 5, 21 December 1957 at Knowsley Road. Back: Glyn Moses, Roy Robinson, Tom McKinney, Abe Terry, Nat Silcock, Frank Carlton, Tom van Vollenhoven, Vince Karalius; front: Austin Rhodes, Ray Price, Alan Prescott (c), Duggie Greenall, Brian Howard.

I remember Tom playing one of his first games for Saints. I was sitting on the bench on the Best Side at Knowsley Road – I was either injured or in uniform, but I was sitting with Joe Egan, the Wigan coach. Vol got the ball and it was the first time he had received it. He had Mick Sullivan opposite him and he just swerved, accelerated and seemed to walk round the full-back Cunliffe. I remember him coming over to the bench and saying "What could I do about that, Joe?" Joe said, quite simply, "Nowt." I think Mick was quite irked about it and stuck one on Tommy after that. Mick Sullivan is also one of the all-time greats, but even he couldn't tackle him.

Tommy had taken Steve Llewellyn's place. Everyone was buoyant, we only had to give him the ball with a little bit of room and it was a try. Defenders were terrified of him. What they had to do was to make him come inside into the cover. If he had the outside, there was usually no stopping him. Billy Boston was a great winger and such a nice bloke. He had perfect timing, great defensive qualities and was a giant of a fellow, immensely strong and so well balanced. Then there was Brian Bevan. I suppose the Wigan fans will have Boston as the greatest and Warrington fans Bevan, but for me, it would always be Tom van Vollenhoven.

Full steam ahead in 1958–59

Tom, together with the signing of second-rower Dick Huddart from Whitehaven after the 1958 Australian tour, reinforced a side that already had power and great pace. Another South African winger, Jan Prinsloo came over to increase our attacking potential out wide. He was as quick as Tom and certainly stockier, but he didn't have Tom's agility, timing or perception. Jan was an out-and-out finisher. If we gave him the ball on the outside, it was all over. He had this tendency of edging into the full-back. They came towards him like a magnet. It's simple to beat a full-back when there is room on the outside.

Needless to say our attack ran riot in 1958–59 and in 38 matches the Saints scored 1,005 points from 215 tries and 180 goals, the most ever registered in the league in a season. Van Vollenhoven broke Alf Ellaby's club record of 55 tries for a season by scorching in for 62. Scrum-half Alex Murphy was sixth in the charts with 37 – a fantastic achievement.

Despite this, the prospect of silverware was not assured. Wigan had won the Lancashire League title – we came second, a point behind – and Oldham had beaten the Saints in the Lancashire Cup Final 12–2. Featherstone Rovers had also ended our Challenge Cup hopes at Post Office Road. I missed both matches because of RAF commitments. We wanted to lift the Championship trophy to cement our top position in the Northern Rugby League table. In those days, of course, a team could finish on top of the table and not win anything.

Towards the back end of the season, we were really struggling for a full-back, with Glyn Moses out of the reckoning with a knee injury. They had tried Peter Fearis there, but obviously it didn't seem to be the answer and before the crucial Championship semi-final at home to Oldham, Jim Sullivan asked me if I would play full-back. I had played in both half-back positions and at centre. I had good hands, so I didn't think full-back would be so difficult. However, I had not played many matches at all during the season, because of RAF commitments and I suppose it was a big gamble on Sully's part. As it happened, we were on fire that afternoon and had a resounding victory, 42–4, against a team that had always been troublesome for us to beat. Ken Large flew in for three tries; Duggie Greenall and Dick Huddart both scored two, and Alex Murphy and Abe Terry completed the scorers. I kicked six goals into the bargain.

The Championship Final was at Odsal against Hunslet. They were a really good side in those days and started well against us – so much so that they led 12–4 at one stage. The little scrum-half, Doyle, with his sidestep, was giving us all sorts of trouble. He scored from a scrum near our line and things were looking quite bleak. His stand-off, Brian Gabbitas, was an outstanding player too. Second rower Geoff Gunney was also a Great Britain international.

'Cometh the hour, cometh the man', as the saying goes. In our case it was Tom van Vollenhoven, who scored the best try I've ever seen. From about 15 yards from his own line he finished up scoring under the sticks and left four would-be tacklers lying on the ground. The stadium erupted and I think the Hunslet team realised that Tom was one man that they could not handle.

Tom ended up with a hat-trick of tries, I kicked 10 goals and in the end we won 44–22. Our score of 44 points was the highest by any winners in all the 43 finals played.

St Helens (24) 44 Hunslet (12) 22
Championship Final
16 May 1959 at Odsal Stadium, Bradford
Attendance: 50,562
St Helens: Austin Rhodes, Tom van Vollenhoven, Duggie Greenall, Brian McGinn, Jan Prinsloo, Wilf Smith, Alex Murphy, Abe Terry, Tom McKinney, Alan Prescott (c), Brian Briggs, Dick Huddart, Vince Karalius.
Scorers: Tries: Van Vollenhoven 3, Prinsloo, Smith, Murphy, Huddart.
Goals: Rhodes 10.
Hunslet: Billy Langton, Ron Colin, Jim Stockdill, Alan Preece, Billy Walker, Brian Gabbitas, Kevin Doyle, Don Hatfield, Sam Smith, Ken Eyre, Harry Poole, Geoff Gunney, Brian Shaw.
Scorers: Tries: Stockdill, Doyle, Poole, Gunney. Goals: Langton 5.
Referee: G. Wilson (Dewsbury)

Eddie Waring said that it was the best Championship final he had ever seen and Vol's try, when we were 12–4 down was also the best. It was the great Jim Sullivan's last match as coach, of course. He was at the end of his seven year contract, and he announced that he would be joining Rochdale Hornets, where he didn't quite have the same impact. He certainly didn't have the talent available like he had at Knowsley Road. Perhaps players are the making of coaches in that respect. Sully was very much the man in charge and he was always watching us. Whenever we played Workington or Whitehaven it was always virtually a weekend trip and we would stay at the Royal Oak in Keswick. One Friday night Brian McGinn and I sneaked out for a drink. It was a glass of Guinness, but somehow Sully found out and came storming into the pub. He was effing and blinding, saying we had no right to be in there, we were professional sportsmen and so on. Although I thought he had a point, he was well over the top nevertheless. Needless to say we had learnt our lesson. Sully was also a brilliant masseur and he tended to concentrate on those lads who were maybe carrying an injury before the match. A man of many talents indeed.

At the end of the season we went on a Welsh tour and played three matches, all against the same team, a Welsh Select XIII. Apparently this was something the club had done in the late 1940s when Saints and Huddersfield also played three games in different venues. They were exhibition matches and very high scoring. The first game at Llanelli on 18 May we won 44–22, the same score as the Championship Final. I scored two tries and kicked seven goals. The other two matches were also high-scoring ones, but I didn't play in the last one. Peter Fearis was at full-back, probably his last appearance for Saints.

My dad and I had always been huge boxing fans and I was thrilled to meet my dad's idol when we went on tour. Jimmy Wilde, the former flyweight, was at one of the matches and I was introduced to him and I told him he was a hero in our household. He told me he had a huge number of fights, something over 600 and he'd only lost two. He said the ref had robbed him on those occasions. Jimmy was getting on a bit by then and was wearing a flat cap and had a walking stick. They used to call him the "Ghost with the hammer in his hand."

Welsh tour 1959
St Helens 44 Welsh Select XIII 22 (Stebonheath, Llanelli)
St Helens 35 Welsh Select XIII 19 (Pontypool Park, Pontypool)
St Helens 47 Welsh Select XIII 31 (Maindy Stadium, Cardiff)

The greatest try I have ever seen on a rugby pitch. After 25 minutes in the 1959 Championship final we were 10–4 down, until Tom van Vollenhoven scored his fantastic 75-yarder. We were back in the match and there was no stopping us after that.

I can understand why Tom van Vollenhoven was maybe just not quite the same after his hamstring injury in the Championship final in 1959. Hamstrings were dodgy injuries in those days and I can vouch for that it is really debilitating. The leg loses its elasticity and is difficult to stretch. The doctor who treated me was the same one who dealt with the top footballers. Denis Law had a similar problem at the same time as I did. Advice on treatment varied, but the best I heard was to keep it stretched as soon as the injury happens and don't rest it. Everyone told me that it had to be rested. This particular fellow said not to rest it. When someone tears their hamstring it is actually internal bleeding. Once that blood congeals, the muscle shortens and gets knotted. Therefore it is important to keep it stretched. I listened to this advice and thought it was common sense. The top-class players of today obviously have the best medical advice and rehabilitation facilities, but the hamstring can still be a troublesome area. Josh Perry, Saints' Australian signing for 2011, had his season ended prematurely by a hamstring-related problem and needed specialised surgery in London to make him right.

I began the 1959–60 season in some of the best form of my career. I managed to score in every game I played for Saints. The team played 45 matches and I took part in 38 of them. We certainly piled on the points in the opening games and I scored tries as well as kicking goals. In the second league match against Blackpool Borough, we won 59–17.

I scored two tries and kicked 10 goals. Needless to say van Vollenhoven chipped in with four – there was no way I could steal his thunder. The following week there was a 21,000 crowd for the visit of Wakefield Trinity to Knowsley Road. They were our biggest rivals from Yorkshire. We ran riot 40–7 and my tally was a hat-trick and five goals. It showed how well the team was playing, of course, but, as shall become clear, there were some matches where the magic wasn't there.

My good form did result in a recall by Lancashire and a trip to Workington to play a strong Cumberland outfit in the County Championship with my team-mate and good friend Dick Huddart at loose-forward for the home team. There were four St Helens players in the Lancashire side, Rhodes, Murphy, Terry and Karalius, and three former St Austin's schoolboys – Walt Tabern, Alex Murphy and me – quite a record for a small school in Thatto Heath.

These matches were always keenly contested and we were beaten 14–8 even though we had more famous names on the team sheet. In Cumberland, that didn't mean anything.

Cumberland 14 Lancashire 8

County Championship

31 August 1959 at Derwent Park, Workington

Cumberland: Joe Hosking (Leigh), Aiden Breen (Huddersfield), John O'Neil (Workington), Eppie Gibson (Whitehaven), Ron Stephenson (Whitehaven), Syd Lowden (Salford), Sol Roper (Workington Town), Bill McAlone (Whitehaven), Alvin Ackerley (Hull KR), Jim Drake (Hull), John Tembey (Whitehaven), Bill Drake (Hull), Dick Huddart (St Helens).

Scorers: Tries: Breen, Stephenson. Goals: Lowden 4.

Lancashire: Austin Rhodes (St Helens), Bobby Greenough (Warrington), Alan Davies (Oldham), Keith Holden (Wigan), Bobby Chisnall (Widnes), Frank Myler (Widnes), Alex Murphy (St Helens), John Barton (Wigan), Walt Tabern (Leigh), Abe Terry (St Helens), Mick Martyn (Leigh), Brian McTigue (Wigan), Vince Karalius (St Helens)

Scorers: Tries: Greenough, Holden. Goal: Rhodes.

Attendance: 5,041

Referee: Eric Clay (Rothwell)

St Helens were still a fantastic team in 1959–60, with Alan Prescott as coach, although we didn't quite manage to hit the heights of the previous campaign. It could be said that we failed on the big occasions. When the Australians came to Knowsley Road, in the match before the first test, we were beaten 15–2, our first defeat of the season, in front of over 30,000. I scored our points with a penalty. It was a fierce encounter, and the referee struggled to keep the peace at times. A few weeks later, we reached the Lancashire Cup Final and played Warrington, who had Brian Bevan in their team.

Warrington were one of the most powerful teams in the league at the time and there was a huge crowd at Central Park. Saints wore their new 'change' kit of black jerseys with a white vee and white shorts – a strip we really didn't like much. It was a game which could have gone either way I suppose, but there was one incident that stood out after about half an hour. I was at full-back and remember the Warrington winger Terry O'Grady made a break and the ball went to Greenough.

He immediately kicked ahead with Bevan in mind. I found myself running towards our try-line with Bevan. Tommy Vol was also with me. I lashed out at the ball to try and kick it dead. I shielded the ball from Bevan, initially. He was behind me and he suddenly did a dive towards the ball and missed it by at least two feet. Then, of course, he jumped up immediately and raised both hands in the air with jubilation, like he always did. His body language said 'I've scored'.

Brian Bevan 'touched down' for the deciding try in the 1959 Lancashire Cup Final. Oh for the big screen of today. Notice the Saints were wearing their change jerseys of black with a white vee.

58

He knew that the referee was a mile away and a try was awarded. His method of celebration was very different from Tom van Vollenhoven, who always seemed to be apologetic when he crossed the whitewash. On that occasion we missed the modern-day 'Big Screen' which would have clearly resolved the issue once and for all. It is fantastic technology and has transformed the game for the better in my opinion.

We also clearly missed Vince Karalius at loose-forward and despite my two penalty goals we couldn't score a try, and lost 5–4. It was just one of those things really. Nat Silcock, who was a former team-mate at Saints, had a real blinder on the day for the Wire.

It was the first time that Warrington had won the Lancashire Cup since 1937. They had been losing finalists twice, and given their strength at that time showed how competitive the competition was.

St Helens (4) 4 Warrington (5) 5
Lancashire Cup Final
31 October 1959 at Central Park, Wigan
Attendance: 39,237

A fantastic crowd of almost 40,000 witnessed a pulsating match, clouded in controversy. Scoring chances were few and far between, with Warrington winger Terry O'Grady keeping his opposite number, Tom van Vollenhoven in check. It was O'Grady who had a major hand in Warrington's decisive try after half an hour, when he made a dazzling 60-yard dash into the Saints' quarter. Stand-off Greenhough took O'Grady's pass and put in a tantalizing grubber kick. Bevan dived to touch down before Vollenhoven kicked the ball away. The St Helens defenders claimed Bevan had missed the ball completely, but referee Matt Coates awarded the try. Eric Fraser converted. Austin Rhodes kicked two penalties for the Saints, who were without charismatic loose-forward Vince Karalius.

St Helens: Austin Rhodes, Tom van Vollenhoven, Duggie Greenall, Brian McGinn, Jan Prinsloo, Wilf Smith, Alex Murphy, Abe Terry, Tom McKinney, Alan Prescott (c), Brian Briggs, Dick Huddart, Fred Terry.
Scorer: Goals: Rhodes 2.

Warrington: Eric Fraser, Brian Bevan, Jim Challinor, Laurie Gilfedder, Terry O'Grady, Bobby Greenough, Jackie Edwards, Nat Silcock, Paddy Lannon, Alastair Brindle, Jack Arkwright, Bill Major, Ally Naughton.
Scorers: Try: Bevan. Goal: Fraser.
Referee: Matt Coates (Pudsey)

We recovered from the loss quite well as it happened and played some great rugby in the league matches. Tom Ashcroft in the *St Helens Newspaper* wrote the following at the end of January 1960: "A question of vital importance for Saints as the season progresses towards its climax is the extent of the demands which the RAF are going to make on the services of Austin Rhodes. I gather that Rhodes will not be pressed into action for Services matches as often as Brian Howard was... Rhodes is such an indispensable link in the Saints machine that he will be sorely missed in the final drive for the retention of the championship title and the cup competition." Kind words indeed. Fortunately, there was no issue regarding the RAF and rugby union.

We had a set-back when Wakefield knocked us out of the Challenge Cup at Knowsley Road, we won the Lancashire League comfortably. I had become the captain, after Alan Prescott had retired as a player and we looked forward to the play-offs and another Championship final.

	P	W	D	L	F	A	Pts
St Helens	38	34	1	3	947	343	69
Wakefield Trinity	38	32	0	6	831	348	64
Hull	38	28	1	9	758	474	57
Wigan	38	27	2	9	828	390	56

Saints were top dogs. Northern Rugby League table 1959–60 top four.

Being top of the table, we played the team in fourth place, Wigan at Knowsley Road. It was a match people still talk about to this day. Is it any wonder why players used to look forward to these 'derby' clashes? There were over 33,000 packed into the ground and it was an all-ticket match. Wigan made what was, I suppose, a 'tactical switch' in moving Mick Sullivan from his normal left-wing position to stand-off, where he was going to mark Alex Murphy.

There was only one motive for that and it paid off. Mick Sullivan was no stand-off, although he was the greatest left-winger I've ever seen play the game. He was put there to cause bother and he certainly did. The two of them had been niggling away for a while until things flared up just before half-time. As Alex rose to play the ball, things got heated and referee Eric Clay sent the pair of them off. Our loss was greater than theirs and Wigan went on to win comfortably 19–9. I was quite upset and fell out with Alex after the match: "Fancy falling for a trick like that," I said, "just because of your ego." In truth, although Alex was a brilliant footballer, he was no fighter as such and I had the impression it was for show.

So there we were top of the pile and nothing to show for it. Wakefield beat Hull in the other semi-final, but Wigan went on to become champions by beating Trinity 27–3. There were 80,000 fans at Odsal – and they always go on about how big our crowds are in the Grand Final at Old Trafford these days. I made a decision to relinquish the captaincy at the end of 1959–60. I always thought that as a last line of defence it was particularly difficult to be an effective captain, even though I used to link up with the attack on a regular basis. It was time for a change. I had a talk with the coach, Alan Prescott and we went upstairs to see Harry Cook. It was an amicable agreement in the end, and Vince Karalius became the new skipper. We all shook hands on it. I wouldn't have had anyone else take over from me. Vinty was a great leader and a true warrior when we went to places like Whitehaven and Hull. A captain's place in those circumstances, as far as I was concerned, was not at full-back.

On a further individual note, I topped the national goalkicking charts with Wakefield's Neil Fox at the end of 1959–60. We both kicked 171 goals, although Neil led the points-scoring charts overall. He had a brilliant season at both club and international level, including a marvellous performance against the visiting Australians in the final test match at Wigan, where he scored 15 of Britain's 18 points. Frank Dyson and Gerry Round were the full-backs in the test series. With the World Cup on the horizon in England at the start of the 1960–61 season, I wasn't over optimistic about making the squad, but as they say: "Never say never." Incidentally, my total of 19 tries from full-back in 1959–60 was later surpassed by Phil Veivers, with 21 in 1989–90.

St Helens RLFC Lancashire League Champions 1959–60.
All smiles at Knowsley Road. I can't remember how I got the facial lacerations,
but it must have been a great scrap. Back: Derek Brown, Bob Dagnall,
Joe Donegan, Brian Briggs, Dick Huddart, Abe Terry, Jan Prinsloo;
seated: Tom van Vollenhoven, Austin Rhodes (c), Alan Prescott (player-coach),
Alex Murphy; front: Brian McGinn, Ken Large, Wilf Smith, Alan Briers.

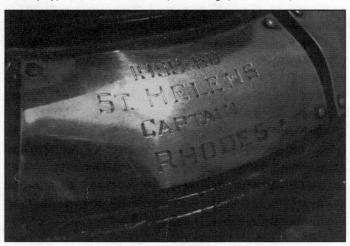

The plaque on the Lancashire League Trophy commemorating
St Helens' Championship and that I captained the team.

8. On top of the world

"Austin was a fantastic player. He had this uncanny ability to step off both feet. I could side-step right to left but not both ways like him. In fact, Sam Tomkins can do it in the modern game. You certainly don't see it very often. The similarity doesn't end there, of course. Sam plays at full-back, like Austin used to do on many occasions, which gives him a bit of protection and he can do a bit of broken field running. For me, he is really a stand-off and Austin could also play in that position with distinction. We played in two World Cups together and ended up winning the competition in 1960. It's always a good feeling beating the Aussies isn't it? Austin was a gentleman. We were great rivals on the field, especially in the Saints versus Wigan matches, but good friends off it."

Billy Boston
Wigan RLFC and Great Britain

The 1960–61 season was one in which we hoped to maintain our position as one of the game's top clubs and bring some silverware back to Knowsley Road after our relative disappointments of the previous campaign. First of all, there was the World Cup to be staged in this country for the first time and I was hopeful about being in the Great Britain squad for the competition.

There was a good chance to impress when I was selected to play for the Great Britain team in a special trial match at Knowsley Road. I had a good game and scored a 60-yard try, as well as kicking a goal. It is incredible to think that there were nearly 14,000 fans there just to watch a practice game. It is interesting to note that Don Devereux was a late choice for the Great Britain team. Unfortunately Vinty Karalius had arrived too late. Punctuality was never his best attribute. Tom Ashcroft in the *St Helens Reporter* said that: "Austin Rhodes, drafted into the senior side in place of the indisposed Eric Fraser, justified an opinion I have long held and expressed that he has no superior at full-back. Rhodes showed his class in the second half when he turned defence into attack and strode straight through the Rest's defence."

The match was played on a Monday evening and a couple of days later I was notified that I was in the squad. Perhaps my utility value also put me in good stead, because I could cover several positions as well as full-back: centre, stand-off and scrum-half. There was also my ability to kick goals.

Great Britain (13) 21 Rest of the League (3) 16
World Cup Trial
12 September 1960 at Knowsley Road
Attendance: 13,500
Great Britain: Austin Rhodes (St Helens), Bobby Greenough (Warrington), Eric Ashton (Wigan), Neil Fox (Wakefield Trinity), Mick Sullivan (Wigan), Frank Myler (Widnes), Alex Murphy (St Helens), John Barton (Wigan), Tommy Harris (Hull), Brian McTigue (Wigan), Don Devereux (Huddersfield), Johnny Whiteley (Hull), Derek Turner (Wakefield Trinity).
Scorers: Tries: Myler 3, Rhodes, Murphy. Goals: Fox 2, Rhodes.
Rest of the League: Frank Dyson (Huddersfield), Fred Smith (Featherstone Rovers), Jim Challinor (Warrington), Alan Davies (Oldham), Ken Large (St Helens 1T), Harold Poynton (Wakefield Trinity), Jackie Edwards (Warrington), Jack Wilkinson (Wakefield Trinity), John Shaw (Halifax), Don Robinson (Leeds), Frank Collier (Wigan), Dick Huddart (St Helens), Brian Shaw (Hunslet).
Scorers: Tries: Davies, Large, Poynton, J. Shaw, B. Shaw. Goals: Collier, Dyson.
Referee: Ron Gelder (Wakefield)

Although we were never actually 'in camp' as today's players would be, we still had a few extra training sessions together at Hunslet's Parkside ground. Bill Fallowfield took the training. I remember talking to Vinty, who had been drafted into the squad despite his absence from the practice match. I said that perhaps it would be a good idea to use one or two of the moves we had up at Saints that I used to orchestrate with some success. "Bugger off, Austin," he said. "Let Fallowfield show us the moves he wants to use. Those are our moves, not for anybody else." I have to say he did have a point. But who would argue with Vinty anyhow?

Great Britain World Cup squad 1960
Eric Ashton (captain/coach, Wigan), Billy Boston (Wigan), Jim Challinor (Warrington), Alan Davies (Oldham), Eric Fraser (Warrington), Bobby Greenough (Warrington), Tommy Harris (Hull), Vince Karalius (St Helens), Brian McTigue (Wigan), Alex Murphy (St Helens), Frank Myler (Widnes), Austin Rhodes (St Helens), Brian Shaw (Hunslet), John Shaw (Halifax), Mick Sullivan (Wigan), Derek Turner (Wakefield Trinity), Johnny Whiteley (Hull), Jack Wilkinson (Wakefield Trinity).

Looking at the make-up of the squad, it is clear that Great Britain were good enough to win the competition, especially with home advantage. We had that hard core of lads who had played in 1957 – Ashton, Boston, Harris, Sullivan, Turner and Whiteley – plus Alex Murphy and Vince Karalius who had been successes on the 1958 Australian tour. As for some of the 'new' faces, there was Jim Challinor from Warrington, who was a big lad, good on defence and could run a bit; his team-mate Eric Fraser was a great full-back who seemed to have the lot; Bobby Greenough was a half-back initially and looking back it was surprising to find him on the wing, but then again, that's why I was selected in 1957, for my utility value. I initially thought that Ray Price was a terrific stand-off, but Frank Myler was a great number six too, extremely strong for his size, with good pace and great for team spirit. Perhaps the one major omission was Neil Fox, a great player. The two 'starting centres' were Alan Davies and Ashton. Maybe Neil was only just starting to blossom into the tremendous player he became.

The forwards were real hard-workers, like Brian McTigue, a magnificent front-rower, who was mobile and extremely fit. He wasn't exactly a flier, but he was durable and a bit of a boxer. That meant that he was a really handy guy to have on our side against the Australians when the going got tough. John Shaw at hooker maybe lacked the overall talent of Tommy Harris, but he was a real hard knock and suited to a dogfight. His name-sake Brian Shaw was a brilliant player, although we didn't often meet at club level, only on international duty. Then there was Jack Wilkinson. I always got on well with him, but he was a real villain on the field. Duggie Greenall used to hate his guts and to his credit I think he worried Duggie on a few occasions – and not many could say that.

Jack was therefore a real asset for our side. I remember talking to Tommy Harris about the Drake brothers at Hull, who I thought were good players. In his opinion, they wouldn't take 'Wilkie' on. He seemed to be the real boss man in Yorkshire.

The 1960 World Cup was between four teams with one league. If there was a tie, there would have been a final. But it was done on a league basis and whoever came top were World Champions. The teams were Great Britain, Australia, New Zealand and France. In reality, whoever beat the Australians would win the cup, but there was no room for complacency in our other two matches.

The 1960 Great Britain World Cup Squad. Back: Bill Fallowfield (Manager),
Brian McTigue, Brian Shaw, Derek Turner, Alan Davies, Eric Fraser,
Billy Boston, Jack Wilkinson, Jim Challinor; front: John Shaw, Austin Rhodes,
Mick Sullivan, Johnny Whiteley, Eric Ashton, Bobby Greenhough,
Tommy Harris, Alex Murphy, Frank Myler, Vince Karalius.
(Courtesy *Rugby League Journal*)

In the first match Great Britain beat New Zealand 23–8 and I wasn't
selected. The backline was Fraser, Greenough, Ashton, Davies and
Sullivan. Looking back, it seems a strange choice to see Bobby
Greenough on the wing in place of the injured Billy Boston. Billy did get
a chance later on though, thank goodness. I remained optimistic that I
could still get a game in the competition. If anyone got injured, I was
the perfect bloke to take their place in the backs.

Australia beat France on the same day at Wigan, although only by
13–12. The French were our next opponents at Swinton and I came
into the team at right centre, replacing Eric Ashton, who was carrying a
knock. On my outside was Jim Challinor, more a centre than a winger,
but he was over six feet and could run. That's the purpose of selecting
a squad for the tournament, when people can fill in when the injuries
happen. The other flank was still Davies and Sullivan. Eric Fraser
remained at full-back and was the appointed goalkicker. We didn't have
the same trouble as the Australians had against the French and we
won quite comfortably 33–7. I scored two tries, as did my co-centre
Alan Davies. Things were often quite volatile with French teams at that
level and sure enough there was some bother. Vinty Karalius was sent
off with one of their forwards, second-rower Jean Barthe. I remember

66

him walking off behind Vinty with his shirt virtually ripped in two. Tom Ashcroft in the *St Helens Reporter* said: "Austin Rhodes had little chance to show his paces until late in the game when he had a hand in a try by Alan Davies. Then he rounded off a Murphy run by cutting through to the posts and was on hand to take Sullivan's pass after the Wigan player had made the only top class wing run of the game."

Great Britain 33 France 7
World Cup match
1 October 1960 at Station Road, Swinton
Attendance: 22,923
Great Britain: Eric Fraser, Jim Challinor, Austin Rhodes, Alan Davies, Mick Sullivan, Frank Myler, Alex Murphy, Jack Wilkinson, John Shaw, Brian McTigue, Brian Shaw, Vince Karalius, John Whiteley (c).
Scorers: Tries: Rhodes 2, Davies 2, Sullivan, Myler, Wilkinson. Goals: Fraser 6.
France: Louis Poletti, Jacques Dubon, Roger Rey, Claude Mantoulan, Raymond Gruppi, Jackie Merquey, Joseph Giraud, Aldo Quaglio, Andre Casas, Robert Eramouspe, Jean Barthe (c), Yves Mezard, Andre Lacaze.
Scorers: Try: Dubon. Goals: Lacaze 2.
Referee: Edouard Martung (France)

Australia went on to beat New Zealand 21–15 at Headingley, which meant that the Great Britain versus Australia game would decide the winners of the title. The New Zealand versus France game was thus irrelevant to who won the competition. It was down to us at Odsal to win the trophy and make amends for our poor showing in 1957.

The good news was that I was selected at full-back for the final and that Billy Boston had returned on the right wing. Unfortunately, Odsal was a sea of mud on the day of the final, with the rain pouring down in bucket-loads. Handling was not going to be easy and the battle of the two hookers was going to be crucial. For all that, my memories of the game itself are a little hazy.

We did enough in the first half to win, with tries from Billy Boston and Mick Sullivan. Goalkicking was not easy given the state of the pitch. I did manage to convert Boston's try in the corner, but the mud and the greasy ball made it extremely difficult to get a good contact. Our forwards worked hard in the conditions throughout the match although we missed Tommy Harris. I thought that our half-backs, Alex Murphy and Frank Myler had great games. Murphy made the break for Mick Sullivan's try and got belted after the ball had gone. I was 'done' that way a few times and was involved in one skirmish on the touchline. I think I managed to get a good right-hander in before getting out of the way. On one occasion I had to pick up a loose ball with two Aussies flying in with their boots. I had to be very quick indeed otherwise I would have probably been knocked unconscious. I remember the Australian centre Reg Gasnier taking the ball thinking that he had an opening and Billy Boston with his usual perfect timing came in off the wing and crash-tackled him. Gasnier screamed blue murder at the player who had sent him the hospital pass.

The Aussies made a break in the first half down our left and I found that I was committed to taking the winger, who had support on the inside. Thankfully Mick Sullivan produced a superb cover tackle and their chance had gone. Sully was one of the all-time greats without a shadow of doubt. In his pomp he was brilliant, with, perhaps only Martin Offiah in later years to come anywhere near him in ability.

Australia pulled it back to 10–3 with Carlson's try in the corner, but the game was won. It is difficult over time to recall who was impressive for the Australians in the match. Gasnier was a great player, of course and always a threat. Harry Wells, his co-centre was quite quiet. Rex Mossop, with his sleeves rolled up for action was forceful. Elton Rasmussen was a strong second-rower, but the one player who certainly sticks in my mind is Gary Parcell. I walked down onto the pitch with him. He even held the gate open for me. 'Go through Austin'. He shook hands with me, but as soon as the game started, his whole demeanour changed and he ended up butting and kicking everybody in a white jersey. There's no doubt that it was a tough game, which would be expected in any game against the Kangaroos, especially with so much at stake. At full-back I was away from most of the rough stuff 'up front', but people still remember this aspect of the match all these years later. Some of the newspaper reports were quite damming, especially from Alf Drewery in the *Yorkshire Post*, who wrote that: "The Odsal match was quite the nastiest it has been my misfortune to report. Some of the players all the time, and most of them some of the time, behaved more like hooligans than international footballers. During most of a sickening second half, anyone within 10 yards of the ball had to expect violent injury being done to him."

Meanwhile Bob Pemberton in the *News Chronicle* took a more sympathetic view. I'm with him, as long as I'm not in the front row: "As soon as the brawn is taken out of rugby league, you may as well play netball with the girls of St Trinian's ... Rugby league is a man's game."

Great Britain 10 Australia 3
World Cup match
8 October 1960 at Odsal Stadium, Bradford
Attendance: 32,773
Great Britain: Austin Rhodes, Billy Boston, Eric Ashton (c), Alan Davies, Mick Sullivan, Frank Myler, Alex Murphy, Jack Wilkinson, John Shaw, Brian McTigue, Brian Shaw, Derek Turner, Vince Karalius
Scorers: Tries: Boston, Sullivan. Goals: Rhodes 2.
Australia: Keith Barnes (c), Ron Boden, Reg Gasnier, Harry Wells, Brian Carlson, Tony Brown, Barry Muir; Dud Beattie, Noel Kelly, Gary Parcell, Rex Mossop, Elton Rasmussen, Brian Hambly
Scorer: Try: Carlson.
Referee: Edouard Martung (France)

There's no doubt about it – 'world champions' has a marvellous ring to it in whatever sport you take part in. We certainly felt very special to have achieved world champions status in rugby league. Looking back it did seem a relatively low key event in that all the matches were all played in the north and Wembley was not used. For us the money was just as important as representing our country. It did help also if our employers were 'sympathetic' to our needs in playing the game. I was a toolmaker at Pilkington's Ravenhead Works and the boss Lord Harry was keen on his rugby. There was never any problem for me. Today we would probably be in camp for the duration of the tournament, with the players being full-time professionals. No worries about knocking off at three and losing two hours pay these days.

Two days later on the Monday I was back at Odsal once again, playing for Great Britain against the Rest of the World. It was a bit of a come-down after the Australia game and instead of 30,000 there were barely 4,000 fans there in that huge bowl of a stadium. I think the game was organised because they didn't have a 'final' as such. We won 33–27 and I kicked three goals. I seem to remember there was a similar kind of match in 1957, but I didn't take part in it.

Meanwhile, after the final we celebrated at a hotel in Bradford and I must confess that Billy Boston bought a large box of cigarettes and started giving the individual packets out. I started smoking and did so for the next six or seven years. When I eventually packed in, it was one of the most sensible things I ever did.

I have been very fortunate to have won all the honours in rugby league with the Saints, including two Wembley wins to go with a World Cup winner's medal. They are all on a par as far as I'm concerned, but in reality, there are not many players with a World Cup winner's medal in their collection.

A right royal occasion

If we thought that our World Cup victory maybe didn't get the praise it deserved, there was to be ample consolation, albeit some 32 years later. A letter came from the executive committee of the Central Council of Physical Education requested the company of Mr and Mrs Austin Rhodes to a Garden Party at Buckingham Palace. It was to celebrate the Queen's 40th year as our monarch and those attending must have achieved world championship status during her reign.

We stayed at a big posh hotel, overlooking Hyde Park. We checked in and were taken to our room. The view was not the best - dustbins in fact. Marlene didn't think it was appropriate and promptly complained. It was almost like 'I'm going to tell the Queen tomorrow if we don't get a better room.' Because she had a bit of a go, they switched us to another room on a higher level that had an amazing view of the Park – a real 'five star' job.

It was a fabulous weekend. At the Palace there was Alex Murphy and Vince Karalius and their wives from rugby league, plus a virtual A-to-Z of Britain's top sports stars. We walked round the gardens and talked to a whole host of people. All the 1966 football World Cup winners were there, including Bobby Moore, Gordon Banks and Roger Hunt. I was snooker mad then and had a chat with Steve Davies. Stephen Hendry was there too, along with Virginia Wade, Stirling Moss and many more. The Queen and Prince Philip walked around and talked to people. The gardens were so big it took us two hours to walk round. Food and soft drinks were laid on and everyone was given an umbrella. They obviously liked to plan for every eventuality. What a fantastic day.

9. Saints at the double

"Austin came out of the RAF in 1959 and had to take over at full-back for us in the Championship Final and did a marvellous job. Then there was the victory over Wigan at Wembley in 1961. He was a good player; you could play him anywhere and he would never let you down. When he went to the World Cup in 1957 he was a scrum-half and when they won it in 1960 he was full-back. Austin was such a confident player and we were really good friends in our early days at Saints. Austin and Marlene and my wife Olwyn and I used to travel all over the place in his black Morris Minor, registration LDJ 285 – Blackpool, Southport, wherever the fancy took us. Not everyone had a car in those days, but Austin did. I was also Austin's best man when he married Marlene at Holy Cross church. Great memories."
Brian McGinn
St Helens RLFC 1959 to 1963

Despite our World Cup triumph there was no respite at club level. The Saints reached the Lancashire Cup Final at the end of October and our opponents were Swinton, who were on the verge of becoming a powerful team. There were almost as many spectators at this match as at Odsal and it was interesting to see if we could win the trophy after the previous year's heartbreak against Warrington at the same venue. I played at stand-off, partnering Alex Murphy, who was scrum-half, with South African signing Percy Landsberg in the number one jersey. Percy was another player signed from South African rugby union. He had excellent hands, but, if anything, his pace let him down.

St Helens (8) 15 Swinton (2) 9
Lancashire Cup Final
29 October 1960 at Central Park, Wigan
Attendance: 31,755
Scrum-half Alex Murphy, on weekend leave from the RAF, and back-to-form winger Tom van Vollenhoven were two of the Saints' stars in the defeat of a plucky Swinton side who never gave up. It was van Vollenhoven who opened the scoring in the 11th minute, with two goals from stand-off Austin Rhodes that gave St. Helens an 8–2 interval lead. Further tries from Austin Rhodes and Ken Large sealed victory for

Leigh 2 St. Helens 15, Lancashire Cup semi-final 17 October 1960 at Hilton Park. Tom van Vollenhoven flies in for one of his three tries. I am on the far right, with Dick Huddart also in the picture.

Lancashire Cup winners 1960–61. Back: Abe Terry, Don Vines, Fred Leyland, Vince Karalius (c), Dick Huddart, Alex Murphy, Austin Rhodes; front: Brian McGinn, Tom van Vollenhoven, Ken Large, Percy Landsberg, Jan Prinsloo, Bob Dagnall.

the red and whites, although Swinton's stand-off Parkinson argued he was inadvertently blocked by referee Eric Clay when he tries to stop Large's surge for the line. Left-winger McGregor scored Swinton's second half try, with captain Albert Blan kicking three goals. Saints' Austin Rhodes added another two-pointer for his team after the interval.

St Helens: Percy Landsberg, Tom van Vollenhoven, Ken Large, Brian McGinn, Jan Prinsloo, Austin Rhodes, Alex Murphy, Abe Terry, Bob Dagnall, Fred Leyland, Don Vines, Dick Huddart, Vince Karalius (c).

Scorers: Tries: van Vollenhoven, Large, Rhodes. Goals: Rhodes 3.

Swinton: Ken Gowers; John Speed, Peter Smethurst, Alan Buckley, Ken McGregor; George Parkinson, Tony Dyson; Bill Bretherton, Trevor Roberts, Dai Moses, Ken Roberts, Peter Norburn, Albert Blan (c).

Scorer: Goals: Blan 3.

Referee: Eric Clay (Rothwell)

We did quite well in the league matches, finishing fourth overall in the main table. Leeds finished as champions, with Warrington and Swinton above us in the top four. Swinton also pipped us by a single point in the Lancashire League. We only lost three matches at home all season, when Wakefield Trinity, Warrington and Swinton beat us in the league. The two matches against Wigan at Knowsley Road pulled in nearly 50,000 fans. I kicked an important goal in the Lancashire Cup tie that helped us to victory.

Those derby matches against Wigan were always special for the players and the fans. More often than not it would be a full house and on occasions they had to lock the gates. The Christmas period was always great for rugby league matches and Saints used to play Leigh and Oldham as well as Wigan. I remember our chairman, Harry Cook, coming into the dressing room one year and saying "You're all on £20 a man to win, and if you win all three, we'll give you £65." That was big bucks in those days. Needless to say we were delighted to pick up £65 at the end of the festive season.

The way to the cup

There were some significant changes to the squad on the flanks before the Challenge Cup deadline. Jan Prinsloo went to Wakefield. I thought he was a great winger and I was a bit surprised the club let him go. He was exceptionally strong and he could fly. He didn't really have a hand-off as such and perhaps he wasn't as alert a rugby player as Tommy Vol, but if his centre did his job and gave him a chance on the outside that would be it more often than not. Apparently he was a 9.6 man for 100 yards on the athletics track back home in South Africa. McDonald Bailey held the British record at 9.6 seconds at one stage.

Frank Carlton, a fine winger and a Lions tourist in 1958, also left and went to Wigan. Mick Sullivan came to Knowsley Road for a world record £11,000 transfer fee. Even though Mick was probably only aged about 27, I questioned the move in some respects. Mick was one of the greatest ever players in the 1950s, who had a tremendous reputation among players and fans, but when we got him, I think he was past his best. However, Mick was a good defensive player and did make some significant contributions in our Challenge Cup run.

In fact, our run began rather disappointingly with Widnes at home, when we could only manage a 5–5 draw. We never really got going on the day, but we murdered them 29–10 in the replay at Naughton Park. Incidentally, the record books remind me that we played Widnes again the following week in the league at Knowsley Road and beat them again, this time 44–7. Tommy Vol scored five tries and I kicked seven goals. I bet they were sick of the sight of us by then.

In the second round we went to Castleford, no easy place to go at any time, and came away with an 18–10 victory. I remember I was under the weather with a severe cold and one of our directors, Sam Hall, bought me a little bottle of rum. "Austin, you'll have to play," he said. "There's nobody else to kick goals." As you know, I was a pretty reluctant kicker at the best of times and Wheldon Road in February is not the easiest place to put the ball between the sticks. There was a howling gale and it was freezing cold. Towards the end of the game, we got a penalty out towards the touchline and I had to go for goal, because the result was still potentially in doubt. When I kicked the ball it swerved all manner of ways and ended up dropping right between the sticks. After the match this bloke came to me and asked how I had managed to weigh up the wind. "I've no idea, cock," I said. "I just gave it a thump and hoped for the best."

Talking about goalkicking, when we were training, Tommy Vol was a brilliant goalkicker, but unfortunately not when it mattered in a match situation. He was terrified. I used to have a bit of fun practising with him and the lads actually called him 'The Boot,' until a fateful day at

Featherstone. I was injured and was limping out on the wing. There was just one point in it at the time and we got a penalty. They asked Tommy to have a go. He put the ball down and his attempt dribbled along the floor. The Yorkshire speccies loved it and quite naturally they gave him a hard time. He came over to me and says: "Rhodesey you can **** off." He was so, so upset. I always rib him about it when I see him.

I missed the next round against Swinton at Knowsley Road, when Frank Barrow, another local lad played at full-back. We then had a difficult hurdle in the semi-finals against a really powerful Hull team who were determined to get to Wembley again after losing in the previous year's final against Wigan. We went to Ilkley for some extra training for the match, which was a bit of a boost for us. Although there was no Vinty Karalius for this game, who was replaced by Fred Terry, we won 26–9. Tom van Vollenhoven scored a superb individual try and Wilf Smith scored two. Our centres, Ken Large and Brian McGinn, scored a try apiece. I scored a try myself and kicked four goals. The crowd was a good one too – nearly 43,000. Hull were a great side at the time, although they still have never managed to lift the Challenge Cup at Wembley even as I write this in July 2011.

Before the Wembley final there was the question of the Championship semi-final, first versus fourth, against Leeds at Headingley. Unfortunately, we lost 11–4. Lewis Jones had a real blinder and Leeds went on to win their first ever Championship final against Warrington at Odsal the week after Wembley. My mate Lewis Jones went on to score a try and kick five goals in the final. As for the Saints team, there was to be one change for the trip to Wembley, with John Donovan making way for Ken Large at right centre to van Vollenhoven. I thought Ken was rather lucky to play at Wembley, but he was a good sprinter and certainly took his chance well. I thought Alan Briers was unlucky not to get the nod – he was a great rugby footballer – a good tackler and he had pace. If John Donovan had played well at Headingley, he would have probably been in the side for the cup final.

Clash of the Titans

Much has been written and spoken about the game over the years and it is hard to believe that we celebrated the 50th anniversary of the contest in 2011. We also looked really smart, with our new red vee jerseys, white shorts and socks. It was the first time that the club had worn this jersey and, of course, you can't imagine a Saints' team playing in anything else these days.

There was a huge build up for the game and it was true to say that there was not that much between the two sides, although as holders, Wigan were slight favourites. There is a theory that the forwards get you to Wembley and the backs win the cup. There might be something in that, but I believe that in the end, the difference was arguably our back three of Vines, Huddart and Karalius. Dick Huddart in particular was a real superstar on the day and was a worthy winner of the Lance Todd trophy. People say I'm daft, that I don't know what I'm talking about, but even Tommy Vol had lost a bit of his devastating pace when we played at Wembley. From when he came to Saints in 1957 to scoring at Odsal against Hunslet in the 1959 Championship final there was no-one to touch him, but that hamstring injury had affected him.

Perhaps the abiding memory was the heat. It must have been particularly bad for the forwards. In the end, we coped with the conditions better than Wigan did. Although I felt drained at times and it was a low-scoring affair, I never really thought we would lose! We were two points down after just four minutes when Wigan full-back Fred Griffiths booted over a penalty. In my role as full-back, I had license to join the attack where and when I thought it was appropriate to do so. Early on I found space on the outside and dragged the centre in and threw a good pass to Kenny Large. I'm sure he must have had an early dose of the famous Wembley nerves, as he failed to make the catch and the ball went to ground. Wigan stand-off Dave Bolton picked it up and there was just the chance that Wigan would capitalise on the error. Thankfully Tom van Vollenhoven was our saviour on that particular occasion, because I was out of position in a defensive sense. Conversely, if Kenny had taken it, he had a two-against-one situation and a try would have been on.

We took the lead just after the half hour, when Alex Murphy got on the end of Dick Huddart's short pass to score a try in the corner. Although I missed the conversion, I kicked a penalty shortly after from just under half-way and we had a 5–2 advantage at half-time. The third quarter was always going to be a crucial time and Wigan threw everything they had at us at one stage. Griffiths kicked another goal to make it 5–4. He missed another effort shortly after to restore the lead, but the major turning point was about to unfurl. As Wigan put us under increasing pressure, I found myself at one stage with both Boston and Eric Ashton bearing down on me. I tried to kid Eric into passing early by shouting "Eric's yours." This was to make him think there was someone about to tackle him. The ploy worked to a degree. Eric did pass a fraction early and Boston went all out for the try line. I managed to get his legs and Brian McGinn, a great defender, together with Cliff Watson, completed the tackle. They would call it scrambling defence today. The referee awarded a try, but the touch judge ruled it out. Mind you, if it was all very much a blur then, it certainly is over 50 years later. The incident would almost certainly have been referred to the Video Referee today, but I think the result would be the same.

From then we rallied and when Wigan lost the ball in our '25', Kenny Large inter-changed passes down the right flank with Tom van Vollenhoven and Kenny gave him the final pass just as Eric Ashton came across to tackle him. Only for his partial obstruction of Eric, Tom might not have scored. I think that Eric would have given up on half-way if Tom had been in his pomp. It was a great try, though and is one of the best ever seen in a Challenge Cup final.

I kicked another long-range penalty goal with under ten minutes to go and, at 12–4, we were definitely going to qualify for that £75 winning bonus. Griffiths kicked another penalty virtually on the final whistle to make it 12–6, but it made no difference. I thought that we were worthy winners in the end.

St Helens (5) 12 Wigan (2) 6

Challenge Cup Final
13 May 1961 at Wembley Stadium, London
Attendance: 94,672
Lance Todd Trophy: Dick Huddart (St Helens)
St Helens: Austin Rhodes, Tom van Vollenhoven, Ken Large, Brian McGinn, Mick Sullivan, Alex Murphy, Wilf Smith, Abe Terry, Bob Dagnall, Cliff Watson, Don Vines, Dick Huddart, Vince Karalius (c).
Scorers: Tries: van Vollenhoven, Murphy. Goals: Rhodes 3.
Wigan: Fred Griffiths, Billy Boston, Eric Ashton (c), Geoff Bootle, Frank Carlton, Dave Bolton, Terry Entwistle, John Barton, Bill Sayer, Brian McTigue, Frank Collier, Geoff Lyon, Roy Evans.
Scorer: Goals: Griffiths 3.
Referee: T. Watkinson (Swinton)

Training at Ilkley before the 1961 Challenge Cup semi-final against Hull.
I get a lift from Abe Terry, with his brother Fred in the background.
(Courtesy Abe Terry & Austin Rhodes)

Wembley 1961: walking out at the famous stadium led by chairman
Harry Cook and captain Vince Karalius.

Three Thatto Heath lads at Wembley! I congratulate Alex Murphy (6) on his
32nd minute try against Wigan. Hooker Bob Dagnall is also
about to join the celebrations.

Wembley 1961: Our captain Vince Karalius shakes hands with the Earl of Derby before the presentation of the Challenge Cup. I look forward to the moment (far right) with great excitement. The man on my left in the suit is Sir Stanley Rous, the president of FIFA.

We're back with the Cup. Vince Karalius hold the trophy aloft in front of a packed crowd at the Town Hall.

St Helens RLFC – Challenge Cup winners 1960–61
Back: Brian McGinn, Abe Terry, Bob Dagnall, Dick Huddart, Cliff Watson, Don Vines; front: Tom van Vollenhoven, Wilf Smith, Alex Murphy, Vince Karalius (c), Mick Sullivan, Austin Rhodes, Ken Large.

Receiving the Cup from Lord Derby was a terrific thrill for us – after all it was the first time we had beaten Wigan in a Challenge Cup final. The welcome back was also amazing. We left Euston, got off at Lime Street and an open-topped bus drove us back to St Helens. It surprised us that so many Liverpudlians cheered us before we reached St Helens. At one point, Vinty got really upset. Apparently there were thousands lining the streets and without any notice the Police said that we had to change our route. Vinty was raving about it. We had a fantastic reception from the fans at the Town Hall and a week later, we took the cup to Knowsley Road before an 'A' team match. The event was filmed by a guy called Ken Walker, a big mate of Vinty's and parts of it appeared on the club's *Farewell to Knowsley Road* DVD in 2010. Most of the players can be seen, including front-rower Fred Leyland, who was on crowd control duty in his Police uniform.

People ask me how it compared to the 1956 Final. It was very similar in fact. To win at Wembley is the pinnacle. In my debut there I helped the lads win the Challenge Cup for the first time in the club's history. On my second appearance under the twin towers, we beat Wigan for the first time and the red vee shirt made its debut as well. I was over the moon on both occasions, to be honest. The difference was the money, £50 to beat Halifax, but we had to pay £15 tax and insurance, so we took £35 home. When we played Wigan, it was £75 and we had to pay £25 tax and insurance. So we came home with £50. It was well worth everything for the pleasure. It was such a great end to what was my best season up at Knowsley Road.

So what made the Saints a Cup winning outfit? I will give my views on the 1961 Wembley team and those who did not play on the big day.

Austin Rhodes – I felt that I was nothing like what I had been two years previously. Injuries had taken their toll and I had lost some pace, but I was still quick enough to do a reasonable job at full-back and I was happy playing there. I was still kicking goals, well over 100 goals and 300 points. I was happy with my game overall, playing in a good side. I played at stand-off in the 1960 Lancashire Cup Final. There were 30,000 at Wigan. I scored a try and kicked three goals. Percy was at number one and I suppose I was really a utility player then, wherever the team needed me.

Tom van Vollenhoven – the best player I have ever seen. He had electrifying pace, a great hand-off, and fabulous body swerve. Brian Bevan was a great winger too, but he couldn't tackle as well as Tom.

Ken Large – although quite slight, he had plenty of pace. He came in to the Wembley squad in place of John Donovan and will always be remembered for his part in van Vollenhoven's great try. Ken and I joined Leigh two seasons later.

Brian McGinn – a great defensive centre, with good hands. He had the lot, except an extra yard of pace. Eric Ashton was a great player, but he never did much when Brian was marking him, home or away.

Mick Sullivan – one of the greatest players of the 1950s, but slightly past his best when he signed for the Saints. I remember him as a team-mate during the 1957 World Cup and he was brilliant. I played against him when he was with Huddersfield. He scored two tries and went round Glyn Moses as though he was a statue. Mind you, he could do that against most full-backs at the time.

Alex Murphy – a major reason why we were such a great side. Alex was on top of his game with fantastic pace and supreme confidence. The fact that he scored 34 tries in the 1960-61 season as a half-back says it all.

Wilf Smith – a great player to have on your side, especially when the going got tough. We were good mates and used to have the occasional drinking session together. I could not keep up with him. Mind you, his father Tommy, who played for St Helens Recs, was good at that too.

Abe Terry – a fine player. At 17 and a half stones he took some stopping. Anyone who has seen the film of him at the SCG when he scored a try from 40 yards out in the third test against the Australians – side-stepped two and went under the sticks – would be impressed.

Bob Dagnall – one of the best hookers in the game. He could guarantee a large percentage of ball from the set scrums, when possession was so vital. Bob had great hands too and is a Saints' all-time great in my opinion.

Cliff Watson – a giant of a man with tremendous power and a lot of pace. He was fearless, but didn't have great hands and was not a great passer of a ball. Vinty Karalius used to get upset with Cliff and didn't rate him initially in terms of overall football ability. He certainly did not stand out with his handling. I was captain at the time and Vinty would complain: "What are we going to do with this fellow, he can be a bit of a liability, can you get him on the wing out of the road?" I think I had to do it on once. Yet he would tackle and he was great at clearing our line, going as far as he could. He was a tower of strength, but he will always be remembered early on for his tackle on Billy Boston in the 1961 Challenge Cup Final. It was a superb cover tackle, but we should also not underestimate Brian McGinn's role in that key moment too.

Don Vines – tremendously strong and he had a better pair of hands than some people gave him credit for. Don was a bit of a showman and of course he was a wrestler too. I did think that he never really got the respect he deserved at Knowsley Road. I found it ironic that before he came all the talk was about the supreme athlete and non-smoker. We were both single fellows and one day he says to me "Where are we going tonight, Austin?" I suggested the NALGO club in Denton's Green. "Pick me up then will you."

Anyhow, I asked this teetotaller and non-smoker what he wanted and he replied "a pint of Guinness and a King Edward cigar!"

Dick Huddart – the thing that made Saints a great side was the back row. Dick Huddart was fabulous – the best-ever forward I've played with. On his day, he was dynamite. He had the power of a forward and the pace of a centre. Dick was a flyer and the fastest second-rower in the game. Dick was so comfortable with the ball in either hand. He would change body direction and switch the ball to his other side and hand-off his opponents with ease. He had the lot. Once a month a guy called Les Howard used to pick us up in a big car and we'd end up in Warrington for a few pints and a Chinese meal. Dick would have another course. We were all sat there bulging, but Dick would say "Same again please." He was great company, as was Vinty.

Vince Karalius - The captain. He was the life and soul of everything at the club. He wasn't as talented as Dick Huddart, but as a player when it mattered, in places like Cumbria and Yorkshire in the winter months, Vinty was the supreme captain. In those days, it was a matter almost of 'kill or be killed' and the conditions were invariably bad. I think I would have backed him against Rocky Marciano. Vinty loved a sing-song and had a voice like a foghorn.

In reserve – John Donovan was unfortunate enough to have a bad game the week before Wembley, otherwise he would probably have kept his place. Ken Large took the number three jersey. Perhaps Alan Briers would have been my selection. Both Ken and Alan definitely had pace to burn, but Alan was stronger and could also play equally well at stand-off. He went on to play there at Wembley for Widnes in 1964, when Vinty was captain. The other player who could count himself unlucky was second-rower Jimmy Measures, who played in many of the matches during the season. He was quick, certainly, but he didn't have the handling ability of Dick Huddart. It was a pity to see him left out and it is probably no consolation to these lads that they would certainly be included in today's '17 man' game with places on the bench.

Coach Alan Prescott – there was some talk about getting rid of Alan during the season, with Jim Brough's name being mentioned. I don't really know how close it got to that. Alan was a smashing lad. The players would have run through a brick wall for him, that's all I will say. Mind you, coaches were not as 'technical' as they are today. It was generally motivation that they specialised in, but Alan could claim he captained and coached the same team to Wembley success. Not many have done that.

10. End of an era

"I never remember Austin being dropped or put in the 'A' team while I was there and that in itself is a measure of his consistency. In his early career as a stand–off there were some good ones running around, like Bolton, Poynton, Archer and no one got the better of him. He didn't fear anyone and I never saw him nervous – the bigger the occasion, the more comfortable he seemed. Austin was never fazed and that was his strong point for me. Austin was a good goalkicker, a fantastic defender and was never afraid to try out different things in attack. There was a documentary many years ago and it showed Saints in the dressing room after they had won the Lancashire Cup [in 1968] and you can hear Austin shout "Eeeehhh... 45 smackeroos." [winning money] That summed him up as well – the ultimate pro."
Jimmy Measures
St Helens, Widnes, Lancashire and Great Britain

Looking back at those days of 50 years ago, they were certainly different in lots of ways. No one could possibly say that we were fitter than the lads of today's Super League, who train most days of the week and have physiotherapists on site and dieticians – you name it. Like many of my generation I was brought up on fish and chips. Mine were usually bought from Howard's in Thatto Heath and were absolutely delicious. The pace has certainly quickened in the modern game. It's actually levelled out and there's not the lightening pace of a van Vollenhoven or a Bevan anymore. We were part-time professionals and it was not unusual to see lads like John Barton from Wigan who would come straight up from the pit and go to Central Park, with his face covered in coal dust. If we didn't play, we didn't get paid and money was very important to us, whatever the level of rugby we played, whether with our clubs or in representative matches.

Talking of representative rugby, I played for Great Britain before I played for my county. When I was selected at scrum-half for the full Lancashire side, against Yorkshire at Naughton Park, Widnes on 23 September 1957, it turned into a bit of a nightmare. I knocked off work early from Ravenhead, got my gear together and caught a bus outside the British Lion in Thatto Heath to Rainhill Stoops. My plan had been to try and catch another bus to Widnes, but, being rush hour, they were full. So I headed off towards Widnes, part jogging, part walking and about half a mile from the ground someone stopped and gave me a lift to the ground. It was only about 20 minutes before kick-off. Swinton's George Parkinson was one of the reserves on the night and I should really have told them the situation – that I had to run most of the way from Rainhill to Widnes and that I was knackered, but if I hadn't played, I wouldn't have been paid. I had already lost an hour's pay from Pilks for knocking off an hour early and then I wouldn't have been paid by Lancashire. In retrospect, I should definitely have 'cried off'.

Lancashire 11 Yorkshire 25
County Championship
23 September 1957 at Naughton Park, Widnes
Attendance: 6,200
Lancashire: Pat Quinn (Leeds), Bill Kindon (Leigh), Phil Jackson (Barrow), Harry Dawson (Widnes), Laurie Gilfedder (Warrington), Dave Bolton (Wigan), Austin Rhodes (St Helens), Alan Prescott (St Helens), G. Murray (Widnes), Brian McTigue (Wigan), Norman Cherrington (Wigan), Jack Grundy (Barrow), Peter Foster (Leigh).
Scorers: Tries: Gilfedder, Prescott, McTigue. Goal: Dawson.
Yorkshire: Frank Dyson (Huddersfield), Alan Snowden (Hunslet), Cyril Woolford (Featherstone Rovers), Mick Sullivan (Huddersfield), John Etty (Oldham), Gordon Brown (Leeds), Stan Kielty (Halifax), Mick Scott (Hull), Sam Smith (Hunslet), Sam Evans (Hull KR), Geoff Gunney (Hunslet), Colin Clifft (Halifax), Johnny Whiteley (Hull).
Scorers: Tries: Sullivan 2, Snowden, Gunney, Whiteley. Goals: Dyson 5
Referee: Eric Clay (Rothwell)

My county debut was further compounded by the fact that Yorkshire beat us 25–11, with two tries from the great Mick Sullivan and I wasn't at my best. Lancashire finished bottom of the County Championship table that season as well. In fact my only other appearance for the county also ended in a defeat, 14–8, when I played full-back against Cumberland at Workington in 1959. Dick Huddart was loose-forward that day for Cumberland and like before, Lancashire failed to win their two matches in the Championship.

Despite the disappointment at county level, the 1961–62 season looked quite promising for me initially, as I was recalled to the Great Britain team for the first test against the Kiwis at Leeds.

Great Britain (8) 11 New Zealand (14) 29
First Test match
30 September 1961 at Headingley, Leeds
Attendance: 16,540
Great Britain: Austin Rhodes (St Helens), Billy Boston (Wigan), Eric Ashton (Wigan), Derek Hallas (Leeds), Terry O'Grady (Warrington), Dave Bolton (Wigan), Alex Murphy (St Helens), John Barton (Wigan), Bill Sayer (Wigan), Brian McTigue (Wigan), Dick Huddart (St Helens), Brian Edgar (Workington Town), Derek Turner (Wakefield Trinity).
Scorers: Tries: Boston 2, Murphy. Goal: Rhodes.
New Zealand: John Fagan, Bernard Hadfield, Reg Cooke, Roger Bailey, Brian Reidy, John Bond, Bill Snowden, Sam Edwards, Jock Butterfield, Maunga Emery, Brian Lee, Don Hammond, Mel Cooke.
Scorers: Tries: Hadfield, Reidy, Edwards. Goals: Fagan 7
Referee: Eric Clay (Leeds)

I must say that New Zealand sides could really be difficult to play against and they really battered us on the day, winning 29–11. I remember instigating a move on the blind side of the pack where I put Eric Ashton away and he ended up putting Billy Boston under the sticks. It was a brilliant start for us, but we were slaughtered in the end. For me, it was tantamount to Custer's Last Stand – they were coming at me from all angles.

I was a bit surprised not to be retained for the next match. Eric Fraser came in at full-back for both the other games, which Great Britain won fairly comfortably and took the series 2–1. It was my last international, as it happened, and my hopes of going on the 1962 Australian tour looked quite remote. I did think I had a chance of selection, but to be honest, I was nowhere near the player I had been three or four years before. Basically the injuries had taken their toll. As it happened, the Great Britain full-back in Australia was Gerry Round from Wakefield Trinity. He played in all the tests, although I think Eric Fraser and Featherstone's Gary Cooper filled in during the short South African tour.

Cup kings of Lancashire

At club level, we once again reached the Lancashire Cup final and came up against our now familiar opponents Swinton. We retained the trophy with relative ease, winning 25–9. My own tally was a try and five goals and other tries came from the usual sources – Murphy, van Vollenhoven, Large and Mick Sullivan.

St Helens (9) 25 Swinton (4) 9
Lancashire Cup Final
11 November 1961 at Central Park, Wigan
Attendance: 30,000
Pace in the threequarter line is an essential pre-requisite for a successful team – provided they are given their fair share of the ball. The half-back combination of Smith and Murphy capitalised on a steady stream of possession from hooker Bob Dagnall to provide tries for Springbok winger Tom van Vollenhoven, his centre Ken Large and bustling left winger Mick Sullivan. Murphy also chipped in with a memorable solo effort, with Austin Rhodes completing an impressive 13-point haul of a try and five goals in an excellent all-round performance. Swinton's try was scored by former Saint Bill Bretherton. Albert Blan kicked three goals. St Helens were far too fast and mobile for Swinton, although the Lions steadfastly refused to throw in the towel.
St Helens: Austin Rhodes, Tom van Vollenhoven, Ken Large, Brian McGinn, Mick Sullivan, Wilf Smith, Alex Murphy, Fred Leyland, Bob Dagnall, Cliff Watson, Ray French, Dick Huddart, Vince Karalius (c).
Scorers: Tries: Rhodes, van Vollenhoven, Large, Sullivan, Murphy.
Goals: Rhodes 5
Swinton: Ken Gowers, Bernard McMahon, Bob Fleet, Malcolm Cummings, John Speed, George Parkinson, Albert Cartwright; Thompson, Trevor Roberts, Bill Bretherton, Ken Roberts, Peter Norburn, Albert Blan (c).
Scorers: Try: Bretherton. Goals: Blan 3.
Referee: Ron Gelder (Wilmslow)

In some ways we thought we were untouchable. That was probably an incorrect assumption. Just because there are some outstanding players in a team doesn't mean that success will come automatically. After winning the Lancashire Cup things didn't exactly go according to plan. The final was on 11 November and we then lost five out of the next seven league matches, including the last three before Christmas on the bounce: away to Hull KR and Wakefield Trinity and at home to Oldham. The board sacked our coach, Alan Prescott after that particular game. There were possible problems if the club did not make the 'top 16' of clubs in the league table, because they were going to form the new First Division for the next season. That is the reason they decided on a

change of coa
not to have
reports from
which we lo
used to be.'
even then a

Things
Karalius di
road too la
the start
He was s
not been
on his ow
circumstan
which suitec
but apparen
Stan McCorm
play' ruling.

A new broom

It is true to say that Stan was an absolute riot, he was hilarious. He was a smashing bloke and had been a great player at Saints, one of my heroes in fact. As a coach, perhaps he had his limitations. We saw the coach twice a week and it must have been difficult for him to get his ideas across in those circumstances, unlike today where they are full-time at Super League level. The board would, on occasions, over-ride the coach if they felt it was appropriate. Jim Sullivan would have had a large input and I don't think he would be completely answerable to the board. Perhaps the circumstances had changed under Alan Prescott. He certainly didn't have the same 'hold' on the directors that Jim Sullivan had. There's no comparison. Alan had only just retired from playing and was still almost one of the boys and this meant that some of the lads were able to have a more relaxed attitude in training. This, coupled with a general air of complacency, meant that things were not exactly what they should have been, given the quality of players we had at Knowsley Road.

St Helens RLFC Lancashire Cup winners 1961. Back: Fred Leyland,
Dick Huddart, Bob Dagnall, Vince Karalius (c), Cliff Watson, Ray French,
Wilf Smith; front: Brian McGinn, Alex Murphy, Ken Large, Mick Sullivan,
Austin Rhodes, Tom van Vollenhoven.

St Helens 2 Huddersfield 13, Challenge Cup Second Round, 3 March 1962
at Knowsley Road. Sheer bedlam in the snow. I look over the prostrate figure
of Tom van Vollenhoven, who has just been stiff-armed by Huddersfield's
Peter Ramsden and is receiving treatment from the trainer. A supporter
has run onto the pitch, showing his anger at the incident.

The side still had a great reliance on the players who had won the cup the previous year. Looking at some of the records, Cliff Watson played the most games during the season, 39. There is no question that Cliff was starting to find his way in rugby league, having come from rugby union. He was certainly limited with his handling ability, but he had electrifying pace for a forward and was as hard as nails. He would batter his opposite number senseless if we told him to. Former rugby union international Ray French, who had come in for Don Vines, played 35 times in his debut season. Don didn't play another game for the Saints after Wembley in 1961 and in my view was sadly missed.

I played 30 times, together with Wilf Smith and Keith Northey, another recruit from local rugby union. Wilf was a fantastic clubman, a real 'salt-of-the-earth' type of character we needed in our team. Keith was a good player with pace and a lovely sidestep. I thought his best position was as a centre, but he played as a full-back and stand-off. He kicked goals with me during the season too.

In the twenties appearance-wise were Brian McGinn on 27, Fred Leyland, 26, Ken Large, 22 and Alan Briers on 21. I thought Alan was unfortunate not to play more matches and I think that for some reason he wasn't as highly rated as he should have been at Knowsley Road. I thought he was a great talent. Vinty only managed 12 matches and looked to be on his way out. A move to Widnes suited him because his business was in the town. The trouble was that he had never been an 'early bird' during his career. The coaches wanted you there at least an hour before kick-off, but this was never the case even in his heyday.

Vinty was replaced at loose-forward by Bill Major, from Widnes. He was a decent footballer, but not really in the same class. There was Keith Ashcroft in the back-row and Frank Barrow at full-back. Frank was a real 'knock-em-down' merchant in his time and a real crowd favourite for his efforts. One of the stalwarts of the past few years also left the club. Abe Terry joined Leeds, which on the surface was an unusual thing for a Lancashire lad to do, but I was also approached by the Leeds club at one time. They asked me to see if I might make the switch, but being a 'stay-at-home' Thatto Heathen I declined the offer. Leeds was almost foreign parts for us in those days.

Dave Harrison was a reliable reserve hooker and to replace Abe Terry, the club signed John Tembey – a good player. He had a fine pair of hands and a decent turn of pace. John commanded the ball and we knew he would create something for us. I rated him highly. One of the surprises of the season was the transfer of Jimmy Measures to Widnes. He was a great running forward with electrifying pace who went on to play for Lancashire and Great Britain after leaving Saints. Alan Briers and Jimmy Measures won Challenge Cup winners medals with Widnes in 1964, with Vinty as captain. That says something.

All part of the game

The 'old' order was changing, for sure and on a personal note I was nowhere near the player I was in the 1950s. The prolapsed disc in my back continued to give me trouble. It was ongoing since 1957. I was also going to St Helens Hospital for cortisone injections in my left ankle and then it had to be strapped up. I played under great difficulty really. I had to keep it strapped up when I played. When I finished playing, it eased off.

I remember the first time the club sent me for a cortisone injection. I was booked in at St Helens Hospital and when I arrived, the surgeon was ready to start. He had this big needle that looked about a foot long and then he asked me those prophetic words "You haven't had anything to eat, have you"? I told him that it was the usual bacon and eggs for breakfast. As you can imagine, he played merry hell with me: "You were told about not having anything to eat before this." Guilty as charged, I suppose. I had a few injections after that, but the ankle was never the same.

My back was my biggest problem by far. I had to be strapped up in the Wembley dressing room by our trainer Norman Borrowdale. It was quite a complicated procedure. It was the same for the World Cup Final. I don't think back surgery was recommended in those days.

We didn't always rely on the top physios and doctors to keep us on the field. I was still troubled with my ankle and it didn't seem to be getting better. I'd had visits to St Helens Hospital to have the ankle manipulated under anaesthetic, but still the problem persisted. Our hooker, Bob Dagnall recommended a guy, I think he was called Seth Lewis, and he said that I should go and see him and he'd fix me up. So I got on two buses to Sutton Park – he must have been a park-keeper there and I met up with him. There I was in the park hut and he said: "Sit down, take thee shoe off and I'll have a look at yer." Anyhow, he gave the ankle a little tug and a tweak and he gave me his diagnosis: "Tha's geet a trapped nerve." He then got some olive oil from a little bottle he had in his pocket and gave the ankle another gentle massage. It was as though the drop of olive oil was worth a tenner. I thought, 'Silly old bugger. He must be having me on.' "You won't feel anything from now on," he said. I asked what I owed him and he wanted 10 Capstan full strength cigarettes. Bob had told me that was his normal request and I had them with me. Anyhow, I jumped on the next bus back to town and went upstairs. I was rolling my ankle round and I kept thinking 'It'll come back soon,' but I never felt it ever again. I'd been having all these injections too.

Meanwhile, in the second half of the 1961–62 season, the team had turned the corner somewhat and the threat of Second Division rugby had well and truly disappeared, although we did finish a disappointing ninth in the table. Our record was played 36, won 23, lost 13 – something that the players and fans had not seen for several years at Knowsley Road.

If we couldn't make a go of it in the league, there was always the Challenge Cup. We were drawn against Huddersfield in the second round at Knowsley Road and were quite confident of beating them. We had won 36–5 in the home league match against the Fartowners a month previously, but there was no repeat of that this time. The game was effectively lost when Peter Ramsden, the Huddersfield loose-forward, floored Tom van Vollenhoven with a terrible stiff arm tackle. The crowd went mad and started throwing snowballs. One of our spectators actually ran on to the pitch to have a go at Ramsden. To cut a long story short, Alex Murphy got involved in the brawl that followed and was sent off with Ramsden. We missed Alex more than they missed Ramsden, that's for sure and they came away with a 13–2 victory. They actually won the Championship that year and were beaten finalists at Wembley. Incidentally, what about Saints' centre-wing partnership that day: van Vollenhoven and Huddart.

My final game of the season at Knowsley Road was against Blackpool Borough. The Saints won easily 37–5, but there was another reason to remember the occasion. Tom van Vollenhoven scored six tries in a game for the second time in his career in a competitive match. The Saints' threequarters that day were as follows: van Vollenhoven (six tries), Briers, Rhodes (three goals) and Northey (two tries, two goals). I was not able to repeat my previous four tries and eight goals performance from the first time Tom scored six, against Wakefield Trinity on 21 December 1957. Ironically I was the only one of his team-mates who had played on that occasion, five years earlier. On Good Friday I was at full-back when Wigan turned us over 12–3 at Central Park, in front of over 32,000 fans. It was to be my last appearance in a Saints' jersey for six years.

Tom van Vollenhoven later improved on his six-try performance in an end-of-season friendly against SHAPE Indians at Knowsley Road, when he scored seven tries and kicked a goal. I didn't play in the match – perhaps that's why he kicked the goal. I would have given him some stick if I was on the field, that's for sure. The visitors were from Supreme Headquarters Allied Powers Europe and were basically rugby union players.

There were rumours about Saints going for a Welsh international during the close season and they came to fruition when the club signed Kel Coslett from Aberavon in July. Kel was a full-back and goalkicker, so I felt uneasy about him being brought into the club. When I first saw him at training, I thought that perhaps there was a certain element of 'work in progress' to be done if he was to succeed in the professional code. He seemed to lack pace somewhat, but was an excellent goalkicker. I did think that he was a threat to me initially, but I had the reputation of being a capable utility player, which was to put me in good stead for the new season. My optimism was soon to be shattered, however.

11. Pastures new

"I was delighted when Austin signed for Leigh. I had already been at Hilton Park for a few years and Leigh were not doing particularly well. They were always a club who would be prepared to splash out every now and again on a big signing in the hope that it would improve the success of the team. I was one and then Austin came from St Helens later on. Austin and I had a great couple of years together. I was at stand-off, with him at scrum-half. We both played full-back a few times too. I suppose we were moved about a bit to play where they thought the team needed it. Austin always gave me the sort of ball that I could use effectively. He was a brilliant player, probably one of the best I've played with. Apart from being an intelligent footballer, he was never short of knocking people about once or twice either. He was my minder in that sense. He reminded me of Mick Shoebottom when I went to Leeds, who was the strong man of the backs. We were all good friends at Leigh and win, lose or draw, we would always socialise afterwards – it was a great club in that way."

Bev Risman
Leigh, Leeds and Great Britain

Pre-season training was going well in the summer of 1962. I felt good and I was looking forward to the new season with enthusiasm. Unfortunately, my world was turned upside down when the Saints' board slapped me on the transfer list. I was very happy at Knowsley Road and never had a fall-out with anyone. It must have been a business matter. The club had signed Kel Coslett from Welsh rugby union, a brilliant goalkicker, but it was still quite a shock to me. I suppose looking back I did sulk initially and I decided that enough was enough and I would retire from rugby. Looking back I feel as though I should have been more pro-active and kept on training, but I didn't and it caught up with me. It was the end of an era at Saints, my good friend Vince Karalius had also left the club. He enjoyed further success at Widnes, and won a Challenge Cup medal in 1964. I rang him straight away for advice about my own situation at Knowsley Road and he said to me "Don't forget, Austin, these are business people you are dealing with and you have got to treat them with a hard-nosed approach." Needless to say those words of advice were very welcome indeed.

Players like us, kids who came from round the corner, the Saints would only offer a pittance to sign on. So I think it was fair that later in our careers, if we did make a success of it, we wanted to be rewarded a bit more. We would go in and ask for a little bit extra, such as a few hundred quid extra for the season. I must confess I did that on a few occasions, but they looked after me and I've no cribs at all with them. At the time of the transfer controversy, I was still living at the family home on Thatto Heath Road and Saints' chairman Harry Cook and club secretary Basil Lowe knocked on the door. They said: "We want you to sign for Leigh". I told them that I was disgusted with the club's stance, putting me on the transfer list after nine years and being treated just like a piece of meat. Another year and I would have qualified for a testimonial. Harry Cook asked if my intentions were still serious about retiring from the game. In the end I told them that I would be prepared to go to Leigh, but I wanted a 'sweetener' of £2,000. 'Cooky' nearly had a heart attack. "You can't be serious, Austin," he said. I replied that I was always serious when talking about money.

This was not the first time that I had 'stung' the Saints for a little bit extra. During the World Cup in South Africa in 1957, I was sitting on the beach at Durban with Eric Ashton and I asked him how much he got for signing for Wigan. Apparently we both got the same figure of £100 from our respective clubs. In my case, the Saints had only offered me £80 originally and I had to push them up another £20. We both believed that this figure was relatively small and I told Eric that I was going to write a letter to the club to see if I could get some more money. When I had completed a draft version of the letter, I showed it to Eric. He was quite enthusiastic about it and asked if he could make a copy. In the end he wrote his version and I did mine, both emphasising the fact that considering our signing on fees, we would be worth quite a lot in the transfer market now. I said I thought it was worth £300. I must confess that I was rather surprised at the reaction. When I got home from the World Cup, there was a cheque waiting for me. I bumped into Eric the following week around town.

"Now, Ash, how did you get on?"

"No problem Austin – £300."

So when Harry Cook put me on the transfer list, he should have really known what to expect. I wanted £2,000. In the end, Harry Cook came round and gave me a cheque for £1,800. I suppose it was money in lieu of a testimonial. Leigh bought me for just over £7,000. The money helped me to buy my house and I was able to put down £1,500 which was a big amount in those days. I used to play golf with Sam Hall, who was a solicitor and a Saints' director. After the transfer had gone through he would always have a joke with me: "How about becoming my financial advisor, Austin?"

To all intents and purposes, I had retired, but in my own mind I knew that it was not really the case. Things ended up back-firing a bit for me. I had wanted a big 'back-hander' and consequently I didn't do any training. When Leigh came in for me, their chairman, Jack Harding said "You've got to play, Austin". I said that I had not trained for two months. In my own mind I thought that if anyone from Saints saw me training, they might call my bluff. When I went to Leigh, I signed on the Wednesday and played my first match the following Saturday, 15 September 1962, against Saints in the Western Division Championship. We lost 20–10 against my former team-mates and I picked up an injury to my hip and lower back. If I'd have kept training, I don't think I would have had the injury, but I put so much effort into a game against my former team. I wanted to make them regret them letting me go. I ended up struggling for a while, but I had to keep going, after all, Leigh had paid over £7,000 for me.

Becoming a Leyther

In retrospect, perhaps it was time to make the break from St Helens, but I had signed for a team who were in the Second Division, although we played some of the top Lancashire clubs in the Western Division Championship, the equivalent of the former Lancashire League. We didn't have the talent like they had at Knowsley Road. The matches we won were only by guts and determination. We didn't really out-class the opposition. I wasn't really happy about the move at first, but I soon realised that they were a good bunch of lads at Hilton Park. It was a change of routine for me, although Leigh had also signed another Saints' player, Ken Large. We shared a lift on training nights. He was a draftsman at BICC and we were good mates. It was the season when so many games were disrupted by the bad winter and for a spell from

Christmas to early March, Ken and I trained at Ruskin Drive in St Helens until the weather got warmer and games were on again.

One of the main reasons Leigh wanted me was on the recommendation of their coach – Alan Prescott, who was my captain and coach for many years at Knowsley Road. He had joined Leigh in January 1962, almost straight after he was sacked by St Helens. Results-wise we struggled during the season. I was seen as something of a utility player and my new team-mates included Bill Robinson, a lovely man, who was in the front-row with the Welshman Stan Owen. Stan was ideal for the heavier grounds in particular. He was fit and had a ruthless will-to-win streak in him. There was also Tony Leadbetter, a former rugby union winger who was signed from St Helens RUFC. His dad had won the *News of the World* Darts championship.

One of the biggest characters was the South African forward Ted Brophy, who had come over to join St Helens a few years before. He would never claim to be the greatest forward ever. He had no pace as such, but he was great for team spirit and absolutely nuts. Ted lived above a chippie in Westfield Street near St Helens town centre and once jumped in the Manchester Ship Canal from the Railway Bridge at Widnes with Alan Winstanley. I saw Ted the day after he did it, funnily enough. I went upstairs to his place in Westfield Street. I said "What on earth have you been doing?" Ted lifted his shirt and he was black and blue from his neck to his backside. He must have turned over and hit the water full on with his back. Perhaps it was a drunken dare, but Ted didn't need drink to do that – he was just daft. I also saw him do a dive at Southport pool off the top board. They cleared the pool for him to do it and there he was just like Johnny Weissmuller.

Ted was actually very light on his feet and worked at a club in Frodsham which I think was called the Mersey View. We used to go there with the Mylers. He would always be asking us if our glasses needed to be filled. He would come over with our refills and more often than not they would be half price. The music would come on and he would do a soft shoe shuffle. Marlene says that he invented the *Moonwalk* before Michael Jackson. He was a very entertaining man and the life-and-soul of the party.

In those days, there were a lot of players who turned out for teams and they didn't have much ability, particularly in the forwards. In the bad weather, ankle deep in mud, they didn't need too much ability.

Side-stepping, swerving and stuff like that were not needed. Grit, determination, size and fitness were the keys to success. They also needed to tackle.

Despite Ted Brophy's uplifting presence, Leigh were pretty ordinary performers in 1962–63. We finished the season in seventh place in the Second Division, winning 14 from 26 matches.

We lost at Workington in the Lancashire Cup and Oldham beat us in the first round of the Challenge Cup at Hilton Park. In the Western Division, we didn't fare too well at all, finishing 11th of 14 teams. We only won one match in the competition. However, things were going to improve at Hilton Park.

A bridge too far

The following season, 1963–64, saw a big improvement in our fortunes. We were still in the Second Division, but in the Lancashire Cup we beat Wigan at Central Park. I scored a try and that marvellous player Bev Risman kicked two goals. It was a real highlight of my stay at Hilton Park. The two sides are great rivals and it was like Manchester United and Liverpool, very intense. Perhaps worse in some ways than Saints and Wigan.

I played at stand-off and seemed settled in the team. We finished second in the Second Division, which earned us promotion, but the RFL went back to one division anyway for 1964–65. For most of the season Terry Entwistle was my partner at scrum-half. Terry was a grafter, who would never let us down. In some ways he was rather unspectacular, no real side-step, or dummy, but a real workhorse and a smashing lad, great for team spirit.

Mick Collins, who played at centre, and Mick Murphy, who was a second-rower, joined us from rugby union. I shared the kicking with Colin Tyrer and Bev Risman. We also had a real flyer on the wing in Rod Tickle. Our team got a settled look about it and we reached the Lancashire Cup Final at Swinton against St Helens. Unfortunately, it was a bridge too far for us. Saints had the firepower, with the likes of Tom van Vollenhoven, who played centre that day, Len Killeen and Alex Murphy and we were soundly beaten in the end after holding them to 4–4 at half-time.

Leigh (4) 4 St Helens (4) 15
Lancashire Cup Final
26 October 1963 at Station Road, Swinton
Attendance: 21,231

A combination of failing to take crucial chances and being eventually ground down by a robust St Helens pack meant that gallant Leigh failed in their bid for Lancashire Cup glory. The Saints sprang a selection surprise with Tom van Vollenhoven at right centre, with fellow South African Len Killeen outside him. Leigh began brightly, prompted by half-backs Rhodes and Entwistle, but could not get the ball over the line. Len Killeen's try just before the interval, which gave the Saints a 5-4 lead was a taste of what was to follow. Vollenhoven and stand-off Wilf Smith scored superb second-half tries. Loose forward Bill Major had a fine game, with Kel Coslett booting over three goals, including one excellent effort from the touchline.

Leigh: Bev Risman, Colin Tyrer, Gordon Lewis, Mick Collins, Tony Leadbetter, Austin Rhodes, Terry Entwistle, Bill Robinson, John Lewis, Stan Owen, Mick Murphy, Mick Martyn, Derek Hurt.
Scorer: Goals: Tyrer 2.
St Helens: Kel Coslett, Len Killeen, Tom van Vollenhoven, Keith Northey, Peter Harvey, Wilf Smith, Alex Murphy; John Tembey, Bob Dagnall, Cliff Watson, Ray French, Keith Ashcroft, Bill Major (c).
Scorers: Tries: Killeen, van Vollenhoven, Smith. Goals: Coslett 3.
Referee: Ron Gelder (Wilmslow)

The County final was a bit of a watershed for us. Stan Owen joined Saints afterwards and Alan Prescott also left the club and was replaced by former Warrington scrum-half Gerry Helme. As for Alan, when he was a player, he was full of guts and was extremely determined. He was supremely fit and was quite ruthless. Yet he couldn't quite make the transition to coach. Alan was a great bloke and lads would play for him because of his reputation. He was a gentleman. It was, perhaps a bit like Jim Sullivan when he moved to Rochdale Hornets – he didn't have the raw material to create a successful side. This was certainly the case when Precky joined Leigh.

In fact, Gerry Helme lasted until Alex Murphy came to Leigh in the late 1960s. He seemed to know a bit more about the game than Alan. There were no real tactics in those days, just a bit of fitness work and maybe work out one or two moves. Precky didn't really do that, he was a fitness fanatic whose idea was to run forward and bash everybody.

Leigh finished 12th in the Northern Rugby League table in 1964–65, and seventh in the Lancashire League. Our improvement continued, although we were defeated in the first round in all the cup competitions. I played the majority of my 27 matches at scrum-half, where I was happiest, with Bev Risman at stand-off. Bev and I became good friends and he went on to captain Great Britain on tour. There is no better honour than that.

In fact, the 1964–65 campaign was to be my last at Leigh. I remember Cliff Evans, the Swinton coach, coming to speak to me after a game and he said that they wanted to sign me. I presumed he had permission to do so. Cliff reckoned that there would be an amicable agreement between the Leigh and Swinton directors. The Swinton chairman Jack Edden signed me for £3,000. He said that I would fit in well with the Swinton set-up. I didn't need much persuading. It was never really my kind of set-up at Leigh, even though I had one or two really good mates there. Rugby-wise, Swinton was the team for me and I thought I could give it a really good go. I think I could say with confidence that Leigh were certainly in a better state when I left than when I joined them, however.

Life with the Lions

I was suffering with the effects of injuries by the time I went to Swinton. I had lost a lot of pace and I thought that at Swinton I would have lads around me who could use their speed and I could use my handling ability to put them into the gaps. There was Ken Gowers who was a brilliant full-back and John Stopford was on the left wing. The two centres, Bobby Fleet and Alan Buckley were fantastic players. Buckley in particular was a flier. At scrum-half there was another flier called Graham Williams. We built up a good understanding. I could do most of the ball-handling and probe – a midfield general in that sense. I didn't have the pace to do damage myself any more. A player may have experience, but it's no good putting other players through gaps if they haven't the ability to take the opportunity through lack of pace.

In the pack was Dave Robinson, a superb loose-forward who later went on the 1966 Lions tour, together with Graham Rees, Derek Clarke, Harold Bate and Ken Halliwell. We really did need some stopping. Yet we just needed that little bit extra, perhaps provided by someone like Frank Foster, who was a natural pack leader. In the winter days, going to Whitehaven, Workington, into Yorkshire, Hull and Hull KR, a team needed fire in the pack. Class in the backs not was not necessarily enough to make a team champions or cup winners, although we were easily a top four side.

I had a great understanding with Graham Rees. I used to stop and hesitate and it looked as if I didn't know what to do with the ball, but it was all a ploy and Graham would then come steaming into the gap. I just slipped the ball to him and he did the rest.

My first season at Swinton was tremendously successful in lots of ways. We finished second in the Northern Rugby League table and in the Lancashire League. The team also had the distinction of beating the Saints at Knowsley Road in the Lancashire Cup – their first home defeat in six years in the competition. We won 8–7 after being behind 7–3 at half-time and Kenny Gowers dropped a goal to win in front of nearly 15,000 fans. It was a brilliant experience. I remember having a go at goal and the conditions didn't seem to be too good. With being a soft-toed kicker I needed to get a proper contact, which I remember I couldn't get for whatever reason – probably the slutch. I remember Gowers dropped his goal with under 10 minutes to spare.

John Stopford always had good games against Saints and he was particularly successful against Tom van Vollenhoven, who would be marking him. Our team was a good one and John got quite a bit of ball. Because he was such a class wingman he would take his chances and there was not much Tommy could do about it. He was Tom's nemesis before that, when he was really in his pomp. Mind you, given how sensational he was when he first came, I thought Tom was just a little over the hill in 1961. If you saw him when he scored against Hunslet and some of the tries he scored against Mick Sullivan, when he was almost still at his peak at Wigan, he would go round Sully like he was a novice.

After beating Saints we lost 4–0 away to Rochdale Hornets in the second round of the Lancashire Cup. Anybody who went to Rochdale in those days invariably found that the pitch was wet and it certainly was not easy for the visitors. A dry ground at Station Road and we would have done them quite easily. The bookies would have given them 15 points start.

102

We got to the semi-final of the BBC2 Floodlit Trophy against Saints at Knowsley Road and lost 9–4. By new year, we were going well in the league and beat Oldham in the first round of the Challenge Cup. The draw for the next round took us to Knowsley Road and we believed we could turn over the so-called St Helens 'Invincibles,' even though we were without Gowers, Speed and Stopford. It was quite tight in the first half and we were in with a shout, but things had gone against us earlier on when Cummings was sent off. I was right by the incident. Tommy Bishop, the Saints' scrum-half, jabbed Cummings with his elbow in the throat and Cummings retaliated with a little slap. Referee Laurie Gant sent him off. It was the usual thing – they only see the reaction. I thought it was a disgraceful decision. I said to Gant "Thanks, sir – you realise that you've just cost us a Wembley place." I thought about taking the lads off the field, to make him realise what he had done and what we thought. I thought it might make him lean towards us a bit, but that never happened. A few weeks later I bumped into him and he apologised, but it was too late.

Easter saw two more matches against the Saints and we won them both. The first win was 20–6 at Station Road and the second a 15–10 victory at Knowsley Road. It was Saints' last home league match of the season. It meant that they had to win their last match at Liverpool City. If they had lost, we would have won the League Leader's trophy and the Lancashire League. This would have been a great achievement, of course, but for me, the trophies that mattered were the Challenge Cup and League Championship. The Lancashire Cup was up there too. In the Championship play-offs, Halifax beat us 33–2 at home. They then lost to Saints in the final, which was at Station Road. "The Lions need a pack to match their attacking potential," wrote one journalist and I agreed. I think we were like Arsenal FC are today – loads of talent and lovely to watch, but just lacking something. But we beat the Saints three times in their famous 'four cups' season.

Beating the 'invincibles': St Helens versus Swinton 1965–66

10/9/1965	LC	Knowsley Road	St Helens 7 Swinton 8	14,500
7/12/1965	FTsf	Knowsley Road	St Helens 9 Swinton 5	9,000
19/3/1966	CC2	Knowsley Road	St Helens 16 Swinton 4	21,119
11/4/1966	Lge	Station Road	Swinton 20 St Helens 6	11,000
22/4/1966	Lge	Knowsley Road	St Helens 10 Swinton 15	13,500

Before the start of the 1966–67 campaign we did our usual pre-season training and began with a match against Saints in a friendly for the Gallie Cup. Despite missing our four Lions tourists who were in Australia, Stopford, Buckley, Gowers and Robinson, we beat them again, 27–13. This was a false dawn because things started to deteriorate in the club's centenary year – and were never quite the same again. We had to take a pay cut and some players were unsettled, such as Graham Williams, who went to Australia. George Parkinson had gone to Rochdale. Peter Kenny and Cumbrian Graham Mackay came on the scene, and Derek Whitehead claimed a place in the squad. We lost to by Oldham in the first round of the Lancashire Cup, although we reached the final of the BBC2 Floodlit Trophy against Castleford at Wheldon Road. I didn't play and we lost 7–2.

We put all our hopes on Challenge Cup success and faced a difficult match against Leeds at Headingley in the third round. We lost a tight match 17–15, in front of a 20,031 crowd. I said to the directors afterwards that I would have been tempted to play Billy 'Daz' Davies and not me. He was my understudy. Even though I had a good game that day and set up a couple of tries for Graham Williams, if we had got any further, they must have picked Billy. My legs were going and I don't think I would have done myself justice at Wembley. The season was over. I remember Ken Gowers didn't play the games at the back end of the season because he was building his house. But we still managed to beat Saints 12–5 as a consolation.

The 1967–68 season showed that our great side was breaking up. We held the Australian tourists to 12–9 at Station Road. It was the last time Swinton played the Australians. Our team was: Whitehead, Reg Williams, Fleet, Buckley, Gommersall, Rhodes, Gowers, Goddard, Cummins, Simpson, Rees, Hutton, Robinson.

Generally it was a disappointing time. We lost in the semi-final of the Lancashire Cup to Saints at Station Road and there was further disappointment to come. Our coach, Cliff Evans had been criticised during the season and a vote of no confidence was passed against him at the club's AGM in December. Cliff, who had been at Swinton since 1954 and won two Championships, later resigned. That was the end of Swinton's great days. Dai Moses, the brother of my former team mate Glyn at Saints, took over as coach and the team lost to Batley in the Challenge Cup first round. By then I had returned to Knowsley Road.

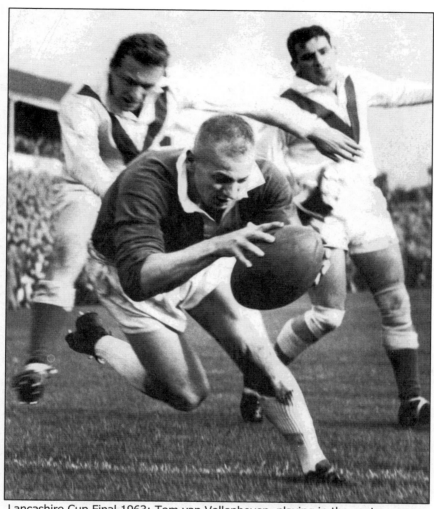

Lancashire Cup Final 1963: Tom van Vollenhoven, playing in the centre, scores for Saints against Leigh at Station Road, Swinton.

A 1963 Leigh team. Back: F. Hewitt, M. Martyn, J. Hodgkiss, W. Robinson, G. Lewis, G. Fletcher, D. Harris, S. Owen; front: A. Rhodes, T. Grainey, B. Risman, E. Gregory, C. Evans; insets: K. Large, S. Walmsley, D. Bridgewater, D. Hurt. The player behind me, Freddie Hewitt, is another Thatto Heath lad. (*Evening Chronicle*)

A trio of Lions – for Swinton and Great Britain. Ken Gowers (far left), Dave Robinson and myself at a Lions dinner.

12. Return of the Saint

"Like Austin, I played a lot of soccer in my younger days and was offered terms with West Bromwich Albion. When I first came to Knowsley Road, the experienced players were a big help when you were trying to establish yourself in the first team. After the four cups year in 1966, the side gradually broke up and we lost the likes of Murphy, Killeen, van Vollenhoven and Bishop. There was a need for experienced players when the club started to rebuild in the late 1960s and that's why Frank Myler and Austin were signed. Frank played more in the centre; Austin was stand-off and he would use his experienced football brain to boss the midfield and dictate the play generally. I remember one game we played together was against Wigan on Boxing Day [1968]. I scored two tries. It was also Bob Dagnall's testimonial match and Eric Ashton refused to let his team continue after half-time and the match was abandoned. We won the replayed match in January though."

Billy Benyon
St Helens RLFC Lancashire and Great Britain 1962 to 1977

I was approaching the veteran stage when the Saints came in for me before the Challenge Cup deadline in 1968 and signed me on for a fee of £1,250. My good friend Frank Myler put in a word on my behalf, apparently, although there was to be a bit of turmoil when I actually returned to Knowsley Road. In a somewhat bizarre twist the coach, Joe Coan, resigned soon afterwards and the club appointed Cliff Evans, who had been in charge of Swinton – the team I had just left. Although Saints had won the Lancashire Cup before Christmas, there had been some criticism of the team's 'forward domination' style of play. I rated Cliff highly, of course and it was a sign that I was really going to enjoy my rugby on my return to my old stamping ground. We had a few hastily arranged training sessions with our 'new' coach, before my first match as a 'born again Saint' in Cumbria, at Barrow's Craven Park on 5 January. I played at stand-off, with Tommy Bishop as my scrum-half. We were both among the scorers. I kicked two goals and Bishop scored a try, but we were beaten 17–7. Not the start I was really hoping for, although things did soon improve. Of the team that played that afternoon, only four were from my first spell at the club:

Frank Barrow at full-back, Tom van Vollenhoven on the right wing, Billy Benyon at right centre and front-rower Cliff Watson.

The full team was: Frank Barrow, Tom van Vollenhoven (c), Billy Benyon, Frank Myler, Les Jones, Austin Rhodes, Tommy Bishop, John Warlow, Bill Sayer, Cliff Watson, Eric Chisnall, Brian Hogan, Joe Robinson. Subs: Johnny Houghton, Joe Egan.

As for the 'familiar faces' their careers had taken different turns since the early part of the decade. Frankie Barrow had made the number one jersey his own and was a real rough-and-tough handful. He didn't have pace as such, but he would knock opponents over and was extremely reliable – a great lad to have on our side in a game, that's for sure. Billy Benyon was just coming through when I had left Knowsley Road, but he had become a fantastic player in the ensuing years. He would definitely have fitted into our 1961 Wembley team. Cliff Watson had become an integral part of the Great Britain squad by the late 1960s. He was a brute of a man, enormously fit and strong with a fair turn of pace. He could never be a 'handling' front-rower as such, but he could stand up to the Australians in the test match arena. Mind you, he could stand up to anybody. As for Tommy Vol, he was certainly not the player he had been in the early 1960s. He had lost some pace and had taken some heavy knocks in the meanwhile. However, he was still a good club-class winger and led the scorers in 1967–68 with 23 tries. The team itself didn't score many points, 472, although our defence was quite efficient, conceding just 334.

Frank Myler played a lot of his games in the centre, with Les Jones outside him. A pacy winger, Les was strong and tough and proved to be very effective during his career. My half-back partner was Tommy Bishop, another Great Britain regular who was at the top of his game then. He was a tough little lad who gave his all. Tommy was quick over 20 yards and difficult to stop. Wilf Smith was still around then and could cover the centre and half-back areas. Alan Whittle was another young lad who could play in the half-backs. He had lots of pace and I developed a good understanding with him. I was the play-making 'veteran' who would put him through the gaps where his pace would do the rest. That's the main thing the Saints wanted me back for, after all.

We had some hard-knock forwards too, like John Warlow, who played in 44 matches in the season. He was a solid, durable player and not many messed with him – just what you needed in the front-row. There was another local-born youngster who was making a big impression. Eric Chisnall was a superb rugby footballer, with an excellent pair of hands and he could fire out a short or long pass if required. He had a bit of pace too – the ideal combination for a successful second-rower. Graham Rees joined us from Swinton shortly after me and he was a great signing for the club. We had a great understanding on the field and he was a superb attacker. He wasn't strong defensively, but he certainly could run with the ball. John Mantle was also in the second-row and was a very good runner and tackler. Not a handler as such, but one of the best-ever signings from rugby union. Unlike Dick Huddart, John didn't have that balanced running style and also people forget that Dick had very good hands and was a good passer of the ball. Like Benyon, John Mantle would certainly have got into our 1961 team. At hooker there was the one-and-only Bill Sayer. A great lad, 'Soss' was arguably past his best when he came to Saints in 1966, but he proved them all wrong. Hookers did not tend to 'age' as much as the rest of us – as long as they could get the ball, that was the most important thing, which he did very well indeed. He was mobile in the loose, enthusiastic and hard as nails – probably my second-choice hooker behind the great Bob Dagnall.

The Saints were arguably in a much better position than when I left the club for the first time – certainly in terms of league position. In 1961–62 the Saints finished in 9th place; Wigan were league leaders. Three Yorkshire clubs, Wakefield, Featherstone and Huddersfield were behind them. After the end of the 36-match programme in 1967–68, Leeds were top with 56 points; the next three clubs, Wakefield Trinity, Hull KR and Saints, all had 49. We were a top four side, albeit by the skin of our teeth. Our points difference was not too good.

We fared much better in the Lancashire League, and finished runners-up to winners Warrington, who beat us to the title by a single point. Incidentally, Wigan finished in 11th place in 1967–68 in the league and it seemed as though the team to beat in the future was Wakefield Trinity, who nearly pulled off a Championship and Challenge Cup double. They lost in the infamous 'watersplash' final at Wembley, when Don Fox missed that last conversion.

It remains one of the biggest disappointments during my second spell at Knowsley Road that I couldn't play in Tom van Vollenhoven's last few matches for the club. He was in his testimonial season and was a real icon as far as the fans were concerned. There will never be another Vol, that's for sure.

One of the biggest problems we faced was the state of the Knowsley Road pitch, which just resembled a sea of mud. Apparently, the drainage system had just collapsed. Our ground at one time used to be up there with Headingley as the best playing surface. Not anymore. When we played Huddersfield in the Challenge Cup, we lost 5–0 and just couldn't get going. The visitors were quite negative in their approach and once they got their five points were just intent on stopping us from playing. Tom Ashcroft in the *St Helens Newspaper* suggested that the inclusion of certain types of players in the team was a waste of time: "Has it been a huge mistake to bring in players like Rees, Myler and Rhodes who are runners and ball-handlers? Would Saints have got an end which would have justified the means if they had concentrated on forward strength down the middle?"

At the end of the season, the club completely revamped the playing surface, bringing in turf from the nearby Grange Park Golf Club to finish it off. There would be no excuses now from the pitch.

Cup kings of Lancashire once again

I felt good at the start of the 1968–69 season and remember making an encouraging start at stand-off half. Unfortunately, full-back Frank Barrow was injured early on and I found myself back in the number one jersey once again. I ended up making 16 appearances at full-back, something I didn't really expect. We started to blaze a trail in the Lancashire Cup and faced Wigan in the first round at Knowsley Road. I scored our second try after 10 minutes and the description of that score in the local paper really did prove what an exciting side we could be on a flat, dry pitch: "Wilson, the Welsh winger, put them on the right track when he took a high ball from Tyrer on his finger tips and retraced his steps on an inner route. Wilson drew two defenders beat one and half got through the second tackle. His timely release of the ball to Benyon, who had taken station on the touchline got the centre on the move. When he had made ground, he switched the move inside by serving the well-placed Sayer and the unerring instinct of Rhodes took him to the hooker's side for a pass which was most gracefully completed with a try at the posts."

It was a great start for us, 16–4 up at half-time. I scored twice, but I was injured by a stray boot and had to leave the field at half-time with mild concussion. Wigan clawed their way back to 16–16 and it was left to Frank Wilson to score the winner about five minutes from time. It was a shame that such a great game was only watched by just over 13,000 people, nothing like the heady days of the late 1950s and early 1960s. Frank Wilson was brought in from Cardiff RFC as Tommy Vol's replacement, which was not an easy task. However, Tom had retired and it was no use looking back. Frank was a good player, strong and fast. He was definitely a good signing for the club and so difficult to stop close to the line.

Widnes fell at Naughton Park in the second round 20–17. Leigh were beaten 17–6 in the semi-final, although I was injured for that one. Our opponents in the final were Oldham, who were not the side I used to play against in the late 1950s by any means, but could not be taken lightly. There was a fair crowd at Central Park, 17,008, and Oldham started well. It was a tight game by half-time, with Oldham leading 2–0. The second half was a complete turnaround and we ran riot. Oldham had injuries to both their front-rowers, Ken Wilson with a knock to his shoulder and Geoff Fletcher with a broken hand, which meant that our big, but mobile pack soon began to get the upper hand, especially in the scrums. Kel Coslett levelled the scores with a penalty and then came the crucial first try after about 10 minutes. The *St Helens Newspaper* took up the story: "Benyon coolly intervened in the opposition onrush, took the ball away to the right and found Rhodes had moved to the critical point of support. Rhodes, who has not long recovered from hamstring trouble, moved like the player he was 10 years ago past the Oldham '25' line and gave Wilson a chance for the corner. The Welsh coloured boy finished the movement with tremendous zest, beating his opposite number handsomely en route."

I remember we scored three tries in as many minutes at one stage, in the 76th, 77th and 78th minutes, and won easily 30–2. Our substitutes, John Houghton and Brian Hogan, were not used. Ironically, later on in the season I would be on the bench and was not called upon to take part in the action, so I know how disappointed they must have felt.

St Helens 30 Oldham 2,
Lancashire Cup Final, 25 October 1968 at Central Park, Wigan.
Back: Frank Myler, Kel Coslett, Frank Wilson, Bill Benyon, Cliff Watson; front:
Graham Rees, Tommy Bishop, Bill Sayer, Cliff Evans (coach), John Warlow,
Alan Whittle, Austin Rhodes, Eric Chisnall, Cen Williams, John Houghton.

St Helens (0) 30 Oldham (2) 2

Lancashire Cup Final

25 October 1968 at Central Park, Wigan

Attendance: 17,008

This was truly the archetypal game of two halves. The Saints were score-less at half-time, with Oldham enjoying a two-point lead. Yet it was to turn around in dramatic fashion over the next forty minutes, with a devastating six try and six goal assault leaving Oldham to wonder what went wrong. They had no answer to the pace of winger Frank Wilson, who notched two scintillating tries and the sheer mobility of forwards Graham Rees and Eric Chisnall, who also got on the scoresheet. Full-back Austin Rhodes, centre Frank Myler and wily scrum-half Tommy Bishop also made significant contributions after the interval. Two Oldham players, Fletcher and Taylor suffered crucial injuries during the match which did not help their cause in the slightest.

St Helens: Austin Rhodes, Frank Wilson, Billy Benyon, Frank Myler,
Cen Williams, Alan Whittle, Tommy Bishop, John Warlow, Bill Sayer, Cliff
Watson, Graham Rees, Eric Chisnall, Kel Coslett.

Subs: John Houghton, Brian Hogan

Scorers: Tries: Wilson 2, Williams, Bishop, Rees, Chisnall. Goals: Coslett 6.

112

Oldham: Martin Murphy, Mike Elliott, Phil Larder, Jim McCormack, Derek Whitehead, Wilf Briggs, Tommy Canning, Ken Wilson, Kevin Taylor, Geoff Fletcher, Bob Irvine, Charlie McCourt, Arthur Hughes.
Subs: Trevor Buckley, Dennis Maders.
Scorer: Goal: Briggs.
Referee: Billy Thompson (Huddersfield)

It was a record eighth success for the Saints in the competition since the war, but, ironically, the club did not win the Lancashire Cup again until Mal Meninga was there, many years later. The game was partly filmed by a BBC camera crew as part of a documentary about the differences between rugby league and union, called *The Game that got away*. It shows the lads in the dressing room being photographed with the cup. I am in a later shot, blurting out "45 smackeroos," – our winning pay – and trying to take a swig from a bottle of champagne. It looked as though I didn't like the taste, but I had forgotten I had a big gash in my mouth. After the celebrations Frank Myler and I came back to the club with John Clegg, who was on the board and was the club's dentist. He said "Come on, I'll take you round to the surgery." He put six stitches in. It must have been those 'eye' teeth of mine again.

The crowds could be quite disappointing in the late 1960s. I can remember playing in front of just 1,500 at Workington the week before the Lancashire Cup Final and 2,500 at Rochdale the week after. One match that did break the 20,000 barrier was when we played Wigan on Boxing Day in 1968. I only played for 40 minutes once again, but for very different reasons. The pitch was absolutely rock-hard and the game should not have gone ahead. I was captain that day and I remember Billy Benyon scored a try and flew into the concrete wall at the Edington End. Before the game, Eric Ashton and I went out to look at the pitch and we both agreed there was no chance of play. I went up to see our chairman, Harry Cook, and told him the pitch was frozen and potentially dangerous, but nearly 20,000 people had assembled and they were still queuing half-way up Dunriding Lane. He said that there was no way the game wouldn't be going ahead. I thoroughly endorsed Eric Ashton's decision to remain in the dressing rooms at half-time and the game was duly abandoned and replayed on 14 January. We won 13–3 and I was on the bench with Eric Chisnall.

We continued to play some excellent rugby, although there were several disappointments as the season went on, including a 4–2 loss to

Warrington at Wilderspool where, once again, we failed to show what we really could do. Bill Sayer lost the scrums to Len McIntyre that day, who was a team-mate of mine when Saints won the Challenge Cup in 1956. At least we were top dogs in Lancashire, in both leagues.

	P	W	D	L	F	A	Pts
Leeds	34	29	2	3	775	358	60
St Helens	34	27	2	5	669	262	56
Wigan	34	25	2	7	732	368	52
Castleford	34	24	2	8	462	255	50

A top four side once more: Northern Rugby League 1968–69

	P	W	D	L	F	A	Pts
St Helens	28	22	2	4	562	220	46
Wigan	28	20	2	6	586	300	42
Workington Town	28	20	0	8	457	266	40
Swinton	28	19	0	9	421	338	38

Champions: Lancashire League winners 1968–69

I didn't realise it at the time, of course, but my final match as a Saint was against Doncaster on 19 April 1969, at Knowsley Road. My memory of the game itself is hazy, but we won easily, 57–2, and I think I did quite well. I played because Tommy Bishop needed further recovery time from a facial injury. There was nothing at stake apart from the winning money. Saints had finished second in the main league table, and had already clinched the Lancashire League title. Before the match, we had a team photograph taken with the two County trophies. The *St Helens Newspaper* helped me to fill in the gaps from the match itself. I played scrum-half and there were only 3,780 present – a far cry from days long gone. The report of the game is most complimentary: "No small credit for Saints' scoring achievement should go to Rhodes. Owing to injury he has been little in the game in recent weeks but he used his return to display all his knowledge to get Whittle moving with well-timed passes in the set pieces and Whittle thrived enormously."

I had lost quite a lot of pace and was now using my hands and football brain to compensate. *The Newspaper* also picked up on the fact that our full-back, John Walsh had enjoyed a great day with the boot, kicking 12 goals: "It was strange that Austin Rhodes, Saints record kicker of all time should be in the side to see this performance."

114

Warrington 4 St. Helens 2. Challenge Cup round 3, 1 March 1969
My last game in the Challenge Cup as a player was a huge disappointment.
Here, I am tackling Warrington's player-coach Peter Harvey as he is about to
off-load the ball. Other Saints in the picture include Alan Whittle (far left),
Tommy Bishop, Kel Coslett and Bill Sayer.

St Helens 57 Doncaster 5, league match, 19 April 1969 at Knowsley Road.
Cup Kings of Lancashire – and my last full game as a Saint. Back: Bill Benyon,
Cliff Watson, John Walsh, Graham Rees, Eric Chisnall, Bobby Wanbon, John
Warlow, John Mantle, Frank Wilson, Joe Egan, Cliff Evans (coach); front: Cen
Williams, Tony Barrow, Alan Whittle, Bill Sayer, Tommy Bishop (c – injured)
Austin Rhodes, Les Jones, Frank Myler. Trophies: Lancashire Cup (left)
Lancashire League.

The Saints team for my 'last hurrah' against Doncaster was as follows: John Walsh, Cen Williams, Tony Barrow, Frank Myler, Les Jones, Alan Whittle, Austin Rhodes, John Warlow, Bill Sayer, Graham Rees, Eric Chisnall, Bobby Wanbon, John Mantle. Subs: Frank Wilson, Joe Egan. *Scorers:* Tries: Barrow 2, Whittle 2, Jones 2, Myler, Warlow, Chisnall, Wanbon, Mantle. Goals: Walsh 12.

It was soon after this match that the Saints made the announcement that skipper Tommy Bishop would be joining the Australian club Cronulla Sutherland at the end of the season, which, of course, would be good for me. The official line was that I was going to take over, albeit temporarily, from him at scrum-half.

Unfortunately, I spent the last few games of the season, including a top 16 play-off match against Castleford, which Saints lost, on the bench. Injuries were certainly taking their toll by this time, but I felt that because of my versatility, I was good to have in the substitute's role. Despite this, I did my pre-season training and things went well, initially and I felt great. I was looking forward to a last hurrah against the top scrum-halves, when I felt a bit of a twinge in my leg. I spoke to the Saints' secretary, Basil Lowe and he told me that the club would send me for an X-ray just as a precaution. The news I received was not what I wanted. The doctor basically told me that I was knackered. I could possibly have gone on for another 12 months, but I would certainly have needed a major operation in two to three years' time. I took the doctor's advice and retired there and then. This was towards the end of July in 1969. I managed to last almost 20 years before my first hip replacement, so it was definitely the right thing to do.

I've since had four hip replacement operations, including two that, shall we say, were not successful. My latest replacement is starting to break up now, but I'll have it done only as a desperate measure. I don't run and no more crown green bowling either. I only want to have a bit of a walk round Taylor Park or the occasional game of snooker.

13. On the other side of the touchline

"When Austin came to coach Pilks Recs, there was no doubt we were already a good side in amateur terms. What he did was to explain some new set moves to us and it certainly gave us even more of an advantage over our opponents. Austin sorted things out and brought more of a pattern to our game. He made us a bit more professional, if you like, and it put us in good stead when we played against the likes of Wigan and Castleford. We frightened the life out of them."
John Forster
Pilkington Recreation 1962 to 1978

It was a bitter blow to realise that my playing career was over at the end of the 1968–69 season. I honestly thought I could have one final season – an Indian summer if you like – at scrum-half. It was just up my street. I had lost virtually all my pace, but I still felt strong enough to be a success in the number seven jersey. I could still knock goals over and side-step. More than anything I was looking forward to bringing on some of the younger players in the team. The succession of injuries had crept up on me more than I had realised and the surgeon was quite adamant that I had no option but to finish playing.

I suppose that I had virtually been a sort of player-coach for several years, especially at Swinton, but it was to be five years before I was given the opportunity to coach professionally. I had no coaching experience at any level, but when Swinton asked me to join them I decided to give it a go. I was appointed by chairman Jack Bateman in June 1974. Swinton had a high regard for me and the feeling was mutual. We had played some brilliant rugby during my previous time there as a player and with players like Gowers, Speed, Stopford and Buckley we had some of the best backs in the league. Perhaps they thought that by appointing me some of my previous success with the club would rub off on the present-day team.

Things were a bit different by the mid-1970s and the club was in the situation of being a yo-yo club between the First and Second Divisions. I had replaced Welshman Rees Thomas, the former Wigan scrum-half, who had been the coach since 1972 and my main aim was to get promotion from the Second Division for the 1974–75 season. I did try to make sure that we played open, attacking rugby for the supporters and improve team spirit generally.

One thing had not changed since I was a player at Station Road – money was still tight, but more so, with the club in the Second Division and with attendances nowhere near what they had been in the glory days of the 1960s. I inherited a team of hardened professionals who weren't necessarily top notch, but they were all big-hearted lads. I was able to get Bobby Fleet, who had been at Swinton when I played there, as my assistant coach and he did a great job at loose-forward for the team. The other lads who were the mainstays included Brian Butler from Swansea, who could run and had a good side-step, but never fully realised his potential. There was Bob Fleay, another Welshman, Graham Evans, Johnny Cooke and Mick Henighan – all good lads and a scrum-half from Wigan called Ken Green. There was Lawrence Lowe, Tommy Young and St Helens-born Kevin Whittle, who wasn't a bad player, but who always thought he had to 'boss' the opposition by retaliating first.

In 1974–75 the bottom four clubs in the First Division were relegated and the top four were promoted. In my first season as coach, Swinton gained promotion to the top flight. We finished in fourth place, with 35 points, three more than Workington in fifth place. It was a really good achievement for us, although we had to beat Batley in the last league match and fortunately put 40 points on them. Huddersfield went up as champions, with Hull KR and Oldham also going up with us.

Although gaining promotion was great, we also did well in the cup competitions and got some notable scalps along the way. In the first round of the Lancashire Cup we were drawn against Wigan at Station Road. They were a top First Division side at the time and ended as runners up to Saints in the league at the end of the season. We ended up beating them 17–15, although the result could have been in doubt but for one vital substitution. Kevin Whittle was involved in a few skirmishes and just before half-time he was warned once more. I knew that if Kevin was sent off we would be struggling. I replaced him with Lol Lowe, who had been champing at the bit waiting for his chance to get on the pitch. The lad had a blinder and we were through to the next round. Unfortunately for us our next match in the competition was at Workington, which was a difficult place to go in the best of circumstances. We lost 17–7 and didn't have the pace out wide to take our chances.

Shortly after our defeat in Cumbria, the John Player Trophy began and we played St Helens at home. To beat the future champions of the First Division was without doubt one of my most memorable achievements as a coach. Bob Fleay scored a crucial try for us and Saints could only manage a couple of penalty goals after half-time. Our 7–6 victory was a credit to the players who tackled like demons for the whole 80 minutes. The team spirit that day was brilliant. We went on to beat Wigan – again – in the second round, 18–2, only to lose against Widnes at Naughton Park in the quarter-finals.

Although we didn't make the same progress in the Challenge Cup, losing once again to Widnes at Naughton Park, our other cup exploits did help us in our league campaign. We also took part in the new Premiership competition at the end of the season. This included the top 12 First Division teams, plus the promoted teams from the Second Division. Once again we did very well, only going down 19–17 to Wigan at Central Park.

The yo-yo syndrome

The chairman was obviously delighted at the club getting promotion and promised funds to help to reinforce the team, but as was often the case at that time, it never happened. I seem to remember that if anything, the side was weakened with the loss of a few players such as skipper Graham Evans, who went to Bradford Northern. At least Bobby Fleet carried on playing, despite retirement rumours and he took over as captain. We did make some new signings, notably front-rower Dave Chisnall from Warrington, but it was always going to be a hard season for us. Lack of money meant that we were unlikely to stay in the First Division. Things came to a head when I offered to resign after seven straight defeats and although they talked me out of it initially, I had left the club by the end of November. I didn't think that I was able to get the best out of the players. Bobby Fleet took over, but it was always going to be difficult and the club were relegated at the end of the season.

Looking up the records, it seems like the position of coach at Swinton was a bit of a poisoned chalice. The next five coaching appointments after me – Bobby Fleet, John Stopford, Terry Gorman, Ken Halliwell and Frank Myler, for whatever reasons, barely lasted over 12 months in charge.

Gaining promotion was a fantastic experience of course, but there had been some tough places to visit. We went to play Huddersfield, Hull KR, Oldham, Workington, Whitehaven, Hull, Huyton, Barrow, Leigh, New Hunslet, Blackpool, Batley and Doncaster. I remember going to one place in Yorkshire and I was warned before we went not to leave any valuables in the dressing room. The lads got changed and walked onto the pitch. I took about half a dozen watches for safe keeping and at the final whistle we returned to find that all the money and the remaining watches had gone. On a personal note I suppose the away trips were quite tiring, together with driving to training on Tuesdays and Thursdays after work. I didn't need the money and it was a chore I found I could do without in the end.

It was probably an advantage having that 'gap' between playing and coaching, unlike, say, Alan Prescott, when he took over at Saints, who was coaching many of the lads who were previously his team-mates. As for me, it was time for a break from rugby matters, although I was later talked into coaching one of the greatest amateur teams in the country – Pilkington Recs.

City Road boys

Ironically, two of my former team-mates at Saints had also coached Pilks before me, Peter Metcalfe and John 'Todder' Dickinson, who were also great half-backs. I was working at Ravenhead at the time and was approached by the club to see if I was interested in being the next coach. I thought I'd give it a go. I inherited a team that was very strong indeed and the club was still closely allied to the Pilkington company. On the surface it would seem to have been a backward step from professional rugby league at Swinton, but the facilities were excellent. They had everything, in fact – great training facilities, a social club and the support of the company chairman, Lord Harry Pilkington, who I thought was a great guy. After some of our successes he would invite all the lads, plus their wives and girlfriends to his home at Windle Hall for a big celebration with him and his wife, Lady Mavis.

Pilks competed in the North West Counties League and there were also the cup competitions which tended to bring the best out of the lads, such as the Lancashire Cup and BARLA Cup for the amateurs and the chance to get drawn against professional opposition in the Challenge Cup, or John Player Trophy if we qualified. The team I inherited had some quality, that's for sure.

There was Peter Glover at full-back, a very solid player who could kick goals; the little right winger Andy Casey, who was great at amateur level; Joey Hull was another brilliant player, a winger with pace, sidestep, chunky in physique – he could go inside or outside his man like a good winger should and a full-back had little chance with him one-on-one.

Then there was Alan Shea, another great player. Rufus Hill was a great footballer too, but lacked pace to play at centre, in my estimation. I think he would have been great at scrum-half. Recs had an international scrum-half in Billy Simmons, who had a tendency to be late getting to the match on occasions. I did plan on Billy not showing up, but it never happened and Rufus stayed in the centre. Loose-forward Sid Wright would also leave it late before turning up and I didn't really want to discipline one and not the other and thus send out mixed messages.

At stand-off was another BARLA international, John McCabe, a great lad who would give us everything. He was a real workhorse, fearless and a great team man. Although he lacked pace as such, there was no-one better for team spirit. Kenny Cross was another international in the front-row. He was a great forward to have on our side when the going got tough and he packed down with the likes of Jeff Gormley, a really mobile hooker, who would dominate the play-the-ball area.

John Forster was another good forward, although he could have done with just a little bit more weight on him. Sid Wright had everything at loose-forward and was another reason we were such a top side at BARLA level. He was a classy player, with a good side-step, a great pair of hands and I thought he could be a bit naughty when the occasion demanded it. I wanted to sign him when I was coach of Swinton. I asked him to come for a trial, but he wouldn't. He was just happy in his own environment playing with the Recs and didn't want the fuss.

"Fantastic, terrific, unbelievable"

The Recs were a top amateur outfit and could really give professional opposition a run for their money. One of the first successes was a 17–0 victory over Leigh Miners Welfare in the Lancashire and Cumbria County Cup Final at Knowsley Road. This enabled us to play in the first round of the Challenge Cup in 1977.

We were delighted to come out of the hat first, which meant a home tie – and ecstatic when the name Wigan came out next. This match captured the public's imagination and was played at Knowsley Road, because our own City Road ground was unsuitable. It was the first time that the Recs had played Wigan since the last season of their semi-professional days in 1938–39, just before they closed down and then the Second World War started. There was huge media interest and I can remember BBC's *Look North* television programme doing a feature on the team.

I felt that the lads had to get stuck into them early on and they certainly did that. We went 2–0 up with a Peter Glover penalty and Sid Wright was just inches away from scoring shortly afterwards. The Recs tackled well until Wigan scored a try from their front-rower Doran. I seem to remember George Fairburn missing a few kicks at goal.

We took the lead once again with another penalty just after half-time and I really thought we were going to get a result. Unfortunately, Joey Hull was harshly penalised at a play-the-ball with about 10 minutes left and Fairburn didn't miss this time. Wigan scored another try with just a few minutes to go, but knew they had got out of jail. Our forwards, Wright, Les Chisnall and Kenny Cross were superb, as were the half-backs, but the whole team tackled like demons.

In some ways we played the better rugby and although we would certainly have settled for a 10–4 scoreline before the match, it was quite disappointing in the end. I asked the lads to go out and die for each other if necessary and they were prepared to do just that. I remember the words of our chairman, Roy Britch, afterwards, that seemed to sum everything up: "Fantastic, terrific, unbelievable... the greatest day in the club's amateur history". Ironically, but for one lucky decision going their way, we would have played Saints in the next round. What about that?

122

Rugby League Challenge Cup Round 1

Pilkington Recreation (2) 4 Wigan (3) 10
Sunday 13 February 1977 at Knowsley Road
Attendance: 11,261
Man-of-the-Match: Billy Simmons (Pilkington Recs)
Pilkington Recs: Peter Glover, Andy Casey, Rufus Hill, Alan Shea, Joey Hull, John McCabe, Billy Simmons, John Forster, Jeff Gormley, Ken Cross, Dennis Colbon, Les Chisnall, Sid Wright (c).
Subs: Jimmy Sheffield (for Hill 40 mins), Alan Speakman (for Colbon 72 mins)
Coach: Austin Rhodes
Scorer: Goals: Glover 2.
Wigan: George Fairburn, Jimmy Hornby, Kieron O'Loughlin, Bill Francis, Green Vigo, Bernard Coyle, Jimmy Nulty, Brian Hogan, Ray Martland, Alan Doran, Kurt Sorenson, Bob Irving, Billy Melling.
Subs: Alan Taylor; Terry Hollingsworth.
Coach: Joe Coan
Scorers: Tries: Doran, Melling. Goals: Fairburn 2.
Referee: Mr Beaumont (Huddersfield)

The toast of rugby league

We won our second Lancashire and Cumbria Cup by beating Latchford Albion at Wilderspool which put us into the Challenge Cup draw once more. I remember we wanted a Second Division outfit to come out of the hat, but we got Castleford – Classy Cas – at home, which meant another big occasion at Knowsley Road and huge media interest.

The lads were not afraid of their opponents and this game was full of great attacking rugby. That was our plan – to take the game to the opposition. We played some brilliant rugby early on and scored twice, when Joey Hull intercepted from about 20 yards and Sid Wright powered his way over. Both tries were converted by Peter Glover and there we were – 10 points up after as many minutes. Cas came back strongly, with their player-coach Mal Reilly leading the way and they scored two tries to get the score back to 10–8. Unbelievably – and this is an amateur team I am talking about – Recs came back with a double from hooker Jeff Gormley, one of which was converted by Glover. It was just before half-time when our luck began to change. Rufus Hill booted the ball up and their winger, Fenton, ended up going the length of the field for a converted try to make it 20–13. It was a definite turning point and they had got themselves a lifeline.

123

Rugby League Challenge Cup
1st Round

PILKINGTON RECS
v
WIGAN

Knowsley Road
Sunday, 13th February 1977
Kick-off 3 p.m. — Programme 10p

Left: The programme for a great day in the history of the Pilkington Recs.

Below: Hooker Jeff Gormley scores one of his two tries as Pilkington Recs frighten the life out of First Division Castleford at Knowsley Road.

In the second half, Cas took the lead with two more converted tries to give them a three point advantage, 23–20, and despite another penalty from Peter Glover, they held out by just the one point. It is difficult to understand that the lads were so disappointed at being beaten instead of recognising that they had lifted the standard of their game to compete on equal terms with one of the best sides in professional rugby league.

The crowd stayed and cheered for quite a while afterwards and the lads did a lap of honour to thank them for their support. The noise during the match was as loud as any I can remember and we had given the Yorkshire lads the fright of their lives. In our dressing room afterwards, Mal Reilly came in and shook hands with all our players and admitted they had been unlucky to lose. He was a gentleman in that respect. If Castleford had been beaten, he may have lost his job as coach, so no wonder he was relieved.

Rugby League Challenge Cup Round 1
Pilkington Recreation (20) 22 Castleford (13) 23
Sunday 26 February 1978 at Knowsley Road
Attendance: 11,000
Man-of-the-match: Jeff Gormley (Pilkington Recs)
Pilkington Recs: Peter Glover, Andy Casey, Rufus Hill, Alan Shea, Joey Hull, John McCabe, Billy Simmons; John Forster, Jeff Gormley, Ken Cross, Steve Smith, Brian Highcock, Sid Wright (c).
Subs: Eddie Fuller, John Finney (for Smith 29 mins).
Coach: Austin Rhodes.
Scorers: Tries: Gormley 2, Hull, Wright. Goals: Glover 5.
Castleford: Geoff Wraith, George Claughton, Nigel Smith, Phil Johnson, Steve Fenton, Bruce Burton, Gary Stephens, David Sampson, Alan Hardy, Peter Cookland, Paul Orr, Mal Reilly (c), Jimmy Crampton.
Subs: Geoff Morris (for Smith 60 mins); Graham Tyreman (for Hardy 40 mins).
Player-coach: Mal Reilly
Scorers: Tries: Johnson, Fenton, Burton, Stephens, Cookland. Goals: Burton 4.
Referee: Billy Thompson (Huddersfield)

The team were crowned Premier League champions of the North West Counties League at the end of 1977–78, another hugely successful season for the boys from City Road. Despite their success, it was not always easy to get the squad together for training, with a lot of the lads on shifts. However, we muddled through and were one of the most successful amateur teams ever. It was a shame that my association with the Recs soon had to come to an end, but I felt that the club wanted a change of direction that I did not particularly agree with and a parting of the ways was inevitable. They were great times at City Road though and I will never forget the success we enjoyed, particularly against the so-called professional big guns. We frightened the life out of both Wigan and Castleford and people still talk about those matches today – they were so proud of the way the team played.

14. Marlene's story

"We have always been a sporting family. Apart from Dad's achievements, I played football and then rugby union when I went to secondary school. My sister Karen was mad on gymnastics and still keeps fit. She has a gym next to her pool in Perth, where she keeps quite a bit of Dad's memorabilia. A little part of St Helens in Western Australia. It's also true to say that the friends mum and dad have made through rugby league have also become family friends, like Frank Myler, the van Vollenhovens and Duggie Greenall. I was particularly close to Duggie. I remember I was doing some shopping one day and all of a sudden, a figure came from my 'blind side,' snatched a loaf of bread from my trolley, side-stepped, sold a few dummies and touched the loaf down at the end of the aisle. Duggie's wife, Vera looked a bit non-plussed by it all. But that was just typical of the man – not bad for someone in his 70s – a real legend."
Martyn Rhodes

I was brought up in Alfred Street, in the centre of St Helens during the early years of the Second World War. I have a sister, Cherrill, who is six years younger than me. I went to Holy Cross primary and Central Modern secondary school in College Street. When I left school I wanted to be involved with anything that involved beauty and I took a job as a hairdresser at Chadwick's salon in North Road. One of my first memories is of my great grandmother, Mary Carson, who was always trying to get small businesses together from her own house. She sold pies to the corner shop and also used to make bread and pop – a very enterprising lady. My mum was also born in Wilson Street and, as Pearl May, became a well-known ballroom dancer from her teens. She started off at the Town Hall and places like Boundary Road baths, when the pool was covered over in winter, and the Co-op. There was always a dance to go to in those days, with the likes of Bert Webb's band playing. It was great at the Co-op with that huge glitter ball on the ceiling. Mum won all sorts of cups and knew all the band leaders of the day such as Joe Loss. She would dance all over the North West, including Blackpool and Southport. It seems difficult to realise, but ballroom dancing was really popular then in the early post-war years

Family circumstances were to change. My mother took a job on at Burtonwood and ended up going to America with a guy called Rod Asher, a Texan, who was in the United States Air Force. She was 40 then and Rod later became my step-father. Cherrill and I initially stayed behind with my nan in Alfred Street, behind the Town Hall. Rod and my mum were based in Nashville at first, but, being in the military, there were postings to different places at various times, such as Turkey and West Germany. Mum went with him, apart from when he served in Vietnam. At that time she stayed with us back home in England for six months and then with my sister until his return.

I had never really had a steady relationship with a boy until I first met Austin at a party in Cambridge Road. I was friendly with a girl called Dorothy Wright and she and her parents knew a few of the Saints' lads. They were big fans of the team. I knew about the Saints, of course, but didn't go to watch them. I was 19 at the time and Austin drove me home afterwards. Unfortunately, he had no idea where he had dropped me off and he later had to ask Dorothy where it was for future reference. We had a few dates off-and-on, but nothing really serious. I did go to the 1961 Challenge Cup Final at Wembley, though. Meanwhile, my mum wanted Cherrill and me to join her in the States. We went to Liverpool and got all the emigration papers sorted out and away we went. I remember being sad giving what I thought would be a final wave to Austin and my nan as we went up the steps to the plane.

We lived at 55 Jay Street in Nashville. Cherrill started high school and I started hairdressing or 'cosmetology' as they called it over there, including facials, nails - the lot. Very posh. It was a good life and I earned rather more than I was in St Helens, but I missed my nan and Austin. After about a year I had saved up and could afford a return ticket. Originally I planned to come back to St Helens for six months before returning to America once more. Don Chadwick, who I had previously worked for, came to see me when I came back and asked me to work for him again while I was over. In the meantime, one thing led to another and I got engaged to Austin and decided my place was in England.

My sister had got married at 18 to a lovely man called Larry Bowman, who had an engineering firm. They lived in Nashville near to Conway Twitty and Roy Orbison. In fact, Larry had a boat and you could see all the homes of the stars from the river, such as Johnny

Cash. They had three children – two boys and a girl – but the marriage didn't work out. Then she married Bill Miracle. He was a good golfer and one of the members at the local club was Tommy Cash, Johnny Cash's brother. Tommy and his wife were invited to the wedding and he sang at it. Both Rod and Bill have since passed away and Cherrill and mum live together in a big house in Hendersonville just outside Nashville. In 2011, Mum celebrated her 90th birthday and I went over to celebrate the occasion.

Austin and I got married on 25 July 1963 at Holy Cross church. Brian McGinn was Austin's best man. The two groomsmen were Wilf Smith, another Saints' player of course, and Danny Sixsmith, my second cousin. Soon we were able to watch our house in Windle being built. When we bought it I remember Vince Karalius saying "You're not paying three thousand pounds for that house are you? That's ridiculous." But with house prices today, it's all relative. In actual fact we were able to pick the house we wanted from the original plan of the plots. We both loved the idea of looking out over the playing fields, with the brook at the bottom of the garden. It's still a lovely spot today and we've been really lucky. We then started a family, with Martyn and then Karen coming along. They both went to the local Catholic High Schools just down the road. Everything seemed ideal and just slotted into place.

When I first went out with Austin I used to go to all the games, but it's true to say that I lost interest when Austin finished. He played for Leigh when we moved here. I used to really enjoy meeting the other players' wives and we had lots of fun, wherever it was, whether at Saints, Leigh, Swinton or Pilkington Recs. I have a soft spot for Swinton because of Bobby Fleet and his wife who used to come over here and visit us. Then there was Bev and Ann Risman and the Mylers were also brilliant company too.

I was never really worried watching Austin play. I always thought he could take care of himself on the field. I never wanted anything to happen to him, of course. I enjoyed everything in connection with his rugby days. It was in his DNA, he loved the training and playing. It gave him so much enjoyment and of course this then made me happy. When he finished playing he took up coaching with Pilks Recs. I remember when they got through to the Challenge Cup first round against Castleford at Knowsley Road. I went to Manchester with Austin.

He was on *Look North* and he was interviewed by Gordon Burns. It was a fantastic game and the crowd were all on the Recs' side. We were invited back to Lord Harry's house at Windle Hall on a few occasions too, which was really special.

From Knowsley Road to the Grand Old Opry

We've come across some famous people on our travels. One time we were going to Nashville but had a few days in Fort Lauderdale. We were on the beach, me, Austin, Karen and Martyn, Rod and my mum and I thought I had seen bandleader James Last nearby. Trust Austin to go over and find out. The next thing he's walking back with James Last. A few months before, Olwyn McGinn and I had watched him at the Guildhall in Preston. I was in awe of him then and now he was in front of me. He picked me up and twirled me round, then he said if ever you want to watch me again there will be tickets for you on the door, just ask – but we never got another chance. One time in Nashville, Cherrill and Larry were filling the car with petrol and Roy Orbison was in the next aisle, with those trademark glasses on. Austin called him over, as he would, and he had such a lovely chat with us. He really seemed to enjoy talking to us. I didn't expect him to be so friendly. We've met country singer Kenny Roberts at the Country Music Hall of Fame and seen Lester Flatt and Earl Scruggs at the Grand Old Opry. We've bumped into Billy Connolly outside the Sydney Opera House too.

Perhaps one of the most memorable occasions was the Garden Party at Buckingham Palace in the early 1990s to celebrate success in British sport. All the 1966 World Cup team were there, including Roger Hunt and Gordon Banks and Austin's day was made because of all the snooker players present. We went with Dave Robinson and his wife but met up with Vince and Barbara Karalius and Alex and Alice Murphy. It was a lovely day and we stayed in a big hotel too. The grounds at the back of the Palace were fantastic and we had cucumber sandwiches and lovely cakes. The Queen and Prince Phillip walked past us. I didn't quite get the sword on my shoulder, but it was a brilliant day nonetheless.

I once did a spot of modelling and took part in a number of fashion shows. I was over 40 when I first started and I ended up doing a lot of assignments with Chris Sudworth, who opened a shop called RARE. Modelling certainly helps to keep your back straight, although I was never one for carrying books on my head to achieve it.

Both our children are a credit to us, but I must say that I was so upset when Karen decided to stay in Australia for good. I cried for weeks. She said she would only be taking a year off and now she is an Australian citizen. But the life she has made for herself makes us both so proud of her. She went there on her own at 20. What a coincidence, I had my 21st in America, hers was in Australia. Our son Martyn also went to live in Australia for a couple of years and Austin reckons I cried once more – because he came back!

Martyn played rugby union at West Park School and was scrum-half when they won the All-England Championship at Preston Grasshoppers ground. His team-mates included Andy and Duncan Platt, Paul Loughlin and Kevin Simms. Martyn has always liked his sport and he helped with the *Question of Sport* series as a member of the 'dummy' panel in Manchester. He started off when David Coleman was at the helm and ended up doing it for 20 years. Before the show itself, they would ask the dummies if the questions were too hard or easy for the celebrity panel. That's where Martyn would meet all the sporting celebrities, such as Frank Bruno and Ian Botham. He works in the financial sector and still compiles the local pub quiz. All in all a rich tapestry of life for Austin and I to enjoy, that's for sure.

Relaxing at Southport in the early 1960s, with Wilf Smith, and Brian & Olwyn McGinn.

Middle and bottom: Extracting Austin's Ford Anglia from the sand at Southport, with Wilf Smith lending a hand.

Our wedding day: 25 July 1963 at Holy Cross Church, St Helens.

Left: A happy family image with our two children, Martyn and Karen in the late 1960s.

Below: On the front at Blackpool in the late 1970s.

Left: "Don't I know you?"
Marlene meets James Last in
Florida.

Meeting Billy Connolly outside the Sydney Opera House in the late 1990s.

Martyn Rhodes and Duggie Greenall at the Saints' Past Players Annual dinner in 2007.

Just part of the job. Martyn meets Ian Botham and boxer Frank Bruno at the *Question of Sport* studios.

A little piece of St Helens down under: Karen and Marlene in front of Austin's Wall of Fame in her gym at her home in Perth.

15. On reflection

"Austin was there right at the beginning when we started the Saints' Past Players Association in the late 1970s and he has remained on the committee ever since. He is just what is needed in terms of a committeeman and is one of the reasons why we have progressed as an organisation, in fact. If he is asked to make an appearance at a forum or a particular event he will invariably be there. The good thing is that Austin can speak in an interesting and informed way about his time with the Saints and about rugby league in general - his opinions are always welcomed – a great lad."

Geoff Pimblett
St Helens RLFC 1971 to 1979
Secretary Saints' Players Association

There have been several matches that I would class as my favourite, such as when we absolutely slaughtered the Australian tourists, 44–2, at Knowsley Road in 1956. I was scrum-half that day and marked Keith 'Yappy' Holman, who sadly passed away in October 2011. The league match against Wakefield Trinity just before Christmas in 1957 was memorable for scoring four tries and, of course, Tom van Vollenhoven going on to get six. Then there was my first Wembley appearance, against Halifax, and my second visit when we played Wigan on that boiling hot day in 1961. The Championship Final in 1959 was a real highlight. Winning the World Cup just has to be the pinnacle, however. There have been disappointments too, such as turning up late for Lancashire's game against Yorkshire at Widnes. I should have told the powers that be to let reserve George Parkinson play instead – but it would have been money lost. Losing in the Challenge Cup at Whitehaven was a big blow. The other major disappointment was for Swinton in the Challenge Cup at Knowsley Road in 1966, when we got a man sent off. We really fancied our chances and the memory still lingers with me to this day.

I used to love playing at Knowsley Road for my home-town team. I liked playing at Wigan too. Saints versus Wigan matches always had a tremendous atmosphere. Then, of course, there was that never-to-be-forgotten Challenge Cup semi-final against Barrow at Central Park – another of the best games I've ever played in – when it was 0–0 at the end of normal time and we beat them in extra time. There were thousands locked out that evening.

People ask me who I would have liked to have played for apart from the Saints. The answer might surprise the diehards, but it would be Wigan. There was such a good atmosphere at the old Central Park and I got on well with the Wigan lads, such as Billy Boston, Eric Ashton and Brian McTigue.

It might have all come to nought, rugby-wise. When Saints put me on the transfer list in the summer of 1962, I could have gone to America to work as a toolmaker in my brother-in-law Larry Bowman's business. It was definitely a possibility at one stage and then I wouldn't have gone to Leigh. These days any transfer dealings would probably have been done by my agent if I was involved in full-time Super League. How times have changed.

As for my most respected opponent, perhaps Reg Gasnier would be pretty well near the top, together with Derek Turner. Rocky was a great player and a genuinely good bloke; Eric Ashton too, although as I have said, Eric didn't necessarily have his best matches against Saints. He never had his greatest performances when he was marked by Brian McGinn in our derby matches. Brian was a great defensive centre. Despite that, Eric was a superb player, like Billy Boston – despite the misgivings of Saints' fans who thought he was never a patch on Tom van Vollenhoven.

The team-mates I have always had the highest respect for are Wilf Smith, Brian McGinn Dick Huddart and Tom van Vollenhoven. Wilf was a great lad to have in any 'hey lads, hey' situation, in the slutch at Whitehaven for example. Brian was a very under-rated player. He had good hands, a complete player in many ways, barring that crucial extra yard of pace. Van Vollenhoven and Huddart were superstars of rugby league. Say no more. In fact, Huddart was tailor-made for today's game; van Vollenhoven too. And don't forget how good the likes of Alex Murphy or Roger Millward would be today. Ability transcends the eras in my opinion, whether pace, handling skills or a good rugby brain.

My favourite position has always been stand-off half. Yet people still remember me just as much as a full-back. This is where I won my major honours in the game, of course and it is not really surprising that I am forever associated with that position. It was quite flattering to know that I received quite a number of votes as a full-back from supporters of a certain generation when they had a competition to name their own Saints' Greatest 17 in 2010. Just for the record, these are my own top 17 team-mates, at club and representative level. It would take a pretty good side to turn this lot over in their pomp, that's for sure:

1 Eric Fraser (Warrington)
2 Tom van Vollenhoven (St Helens)
3 Eric Ashton (Wigan, c)
4 Brian McGinn (St Helens)
5 Mick Sullivan (Wigan & St Helens)
6 Frank Myler (Widnes & St Helens)
7 Alex Murphy (St Helens)
8 Abe Terry (St Helens)
9 Bob Dagnall (St Helens)
10 Brian McTigue (Wigan)
11 Dave Robinson (Swinton)
12 Dick Huddart (St Helens)
13 Vince Karalius (St Helens)
Interchange bench:
Billy Boston (Wigan)
Ray Price (St Helens)
Nat Silcock (St Helens)
Derek Turner (Oldham & Wakefield Trinity)
Coach: Jim Sullivan (St Helens)

Same old game?

People often ask would I like to play in modern-day Super League? Of course I would. Perhaps with advances in surgery, I would have had fewer long-term injury problems. I would be at scrum-half or stand-off, at first receiver, working moves just like I did at Saints and, particularly, at Swinton. I had a terrific understanding with Bobby Fleet, Alan Buckley, Graham Williams and Graham Rees that was honed on the training pitch. Imagine how good we would have been training full-time? These lads would still be great today. The game's still about handling and pace – Buckley had good hands and pace – so these are still important factors. But we would all be fitter, stronger and faster by training full-time. My diet would also be better today. I used to have to go to work six days a week and very often on Sundays for extra money. If we were playing at Knowsley Road I used to clock off at 12 midday, have an egg and a piece of steak, and then walk up to the ground just in time for the match. How different is that from today? How can we compete with what these fellows have today? It's a whole new ball game.

There is a theory that there are no real fliers in the game these days and that the pace has evened itself out. Don't forget that the likes of van Vollenhoven and Prinsloo were rugby players and accomplished sprinters in the summer months back in South Africa. It would be interesting to see what today's players could do on the athletics track in the 100 metres. I think they would go some to match Prinsloo's 9.6 seconds personal best for the 100 yards.

As a kicker myself, it was great to see Jamie Foster kicking a goal from half-way in the Grand Final at Old Trafford in 2011, but modern match-balls are lighter and they use kicking tees. We used to have to dig our own holes to place the ball ready for the kick. It was considerably different in the mud of winter. The film of the 1960 World Cup against Australia shows that the ball I am trying to kick can hardly be seen. I was never one for too much preparation, polishing the ball or excavating a hole in the pitch to place the ball. I used to just want to get it over with. Some kickers had hard toes in their boots, such as Kel Coslett. I always wore soft leather toed boots. Toe caps would have inhibited my movement and ability to step, which was very important to me.

I remember looking at an autobiography of a famous football player, called Len Shackleton, who played for Sunderland and Newcastle. One page was left completely blank because it was supposed to be what the average director of a club knew about football. Perhaps I could see where he was coming from, but generally speaking there were board members at Knowsley Road who had an excellent knowledge of the game, such as chairman Harry Cook. I found another director, Sam Hall to be extremely knowledgeable, as was Lionel Swift, who used to watch all our schoolboy matches and certainly spoke a lot of sense. There were one or two who maybe didn't impress too much, but Harry Cook would have kept them in order. Don't forget, in those days the coach picked the team and the board had the final say. I don't think they would have done with Jim Sullivan, but it was the norm at the time.

When I was no longer playing or coaching, I was there at the start of Saints' Past Players in the late 1970s and as an organisation it has come on in leaps and bounds since then. Geoff Pimblett, the secretary, in particular does a magnificent job and the annual dinners are always superb affairs. I don't think I've missed one. It is great to keep in touch with former team-mates and opponents and we always have several different functions during the year, including a trip to the Grand Final, which has had added interest with the Saints' recent involvement in matches there.

Sport for all

When I finished playing rugby league I still took a keen interest in both watching and playing sport. I've loved sport all my life – rugby league, football, boxing, snooker, crown green bowling, golf, bring them on. Frank Myler was a good golfing companion for many years and I was a member at the Grange Park and Haydock clubs for a long time. Alex Murphy and I challenged some footballers one time, including Ian St John and came away with the money. We've been to numerous Open Championships and saw Tony Jacklin win the Open. One of my favourite golfers was Lee Trevino. He was always entertaining, and always talking on the tee. Then there was Gary Player and Jack Nicklaus, two brilliant golfers in their own right.

I like boxing and there was a time when the Nigerian featherweight Hogan 'Kid' Bassey, who later got the MBE, trained privately at Lowe House gym in St Helens with his trainer Charlie Fox. I was a good friend of Albert Freeman who boxed at Lowe House and I occasionally trained there along with the McNamara brothers. When we heard of the fight between Bassey and the French Algerian Cherrif Hamia taking place at Harringay Arena, we decided to go to the fight and combine it with a few days in London. It just so happened that we were on the same train as Bassey and Charlie Fox. My mate Albert knew Charlie and we finished up in their company on the way down, which obviously added to the excitement. The 'Kid' from Nigeria had previously beaten Hamia to win the Empire featherweight Championship in Paris in 1957. He retained his title that night in London by a knockout.

I like watching track and field athletics. What about Kelly Holmes and her two Olympic gold medals? Fantastic. We've watched test match cricket too and there was no better feeling than when England won the Ashes in 2005. The last-ditch battle between Warne and Flintoff made me into a real bag of nerves. We've watched games at Lords and at the WACA ground in Perth. It was a terrific thrill in the 1957 World Cup to get changed at the Sydney Cricket ground, where we were in the same place as Don Bradman had played. You just can't beat that. We were at the WACA when both the Waugh brothers got centuries. Ramprakash got 75 and had a good knock, but Glenn McGrath was terrific and helped Australia to win against England.

Steve Davis used to be my favourite snooker player and we had great fun watching the championships at the Crucible in Sheffield. There was Higgins, Jimmy White – all great characters and fantastic players. Then there was Tommy Poulding's pub, the Cherry Tree, in St Helens, where we had some great times. There were snooker exhibitions and some serious competitions held there. Some of the professionals who played there included Terry Griffiths, John Parrot and Ray Reardon.

Crown green bowls was another interest; I've beaten a few good 'uns in my time, such as Bert Finch at the Alexandra green in Crossley Road. He'd just won the Isle of Man Open. Thatto Heath had some great crown green bowlers, such as 'Nailly' Pennington, Frank Waterworth, Bob Gee, all the top bowlers in the county. The bowling green at the 'Alex' was a magnificent and a fantastic venue.

With my family connections, it has meant that we have had some memorable trips to America and Australia. So I've been lucky enough to see quite a bit of the world. Rugby has obviously shaped my life and I don't really know what I would have done without it. I might have been a better snooker and crown green player for sure. I may have had a career in football. I was inside-right at school, a striker in modern-day parlance, and it would have been great to have worn an Everton jersey at Goodison Park – a far cry from Toll Bar Congs.

Overall, I would change very little about my life and I have a wonderful wife and family. But if push came to shove, there would be one thing I would definitely change – doing those damn weights all those years ago.

Celebrating Harry Cook's 90th birthday with some of Saints' greatest-ever players. Left to right: Alan Prescott, Bob Dagnall, Austin Rhodes, Duggie Greenall, Glyn Moses, Harry Cook (cutting cake), Stan McCormick, Eric Chisnall, Billy Benyon, George Nicholls, John Mantle.
Front: Alex Murphy, Peter Harvey.

Three Challenge Cup winners from 1961. Rhodes, McGinn and Smith.

Opening an exhibition at the World of Glass in St Helens in 2001. I chatted to former Manchester United star Bill Foulkes about his father, who was a champion crown green bowler. Left to right: Austin Rhodes, Wilf Smith, Frank Barrow, Bill Foulkes, Keith Northey, Geoff Pimblett, Peter Harvey.

Welcoming back Dick Huddart on one of his rare visits back to England, in 2004. Back: Brian McGinn, Wilf Smith, Glyn Moses, Bill Knowles, Arthur Pimblett, Austin Rhodes, Dick Huddart, Keith Northey, Ray French, Jim Measures; front: Peter Harvey, Duggie Greenall, Fred Terry, Abe Terry.

144

Top: On the dunes at Southport with Wilf Smith. Bottom: over 40 years later, presenting him with his portrait after his induction into the Saints' Past Players' Hall of Fame in 2004.

Launching Saints' new heritage jersey at Knowsley Road in 2010, with (from left) Peter Harvey, Kel Coslett, Paul Sculthorpe and Geoff Pimblett. (Bernard Platt)

Best of friends. Having a pint with Tom van Vollenhoven during one of his first visits back to England in the late 1970s.

16. The last word

I first met Austin in 1957, just after he had come back from the World Cup with Great Britain. I have only the highest regard for him as a person and a player. Let me say this: if I was back at school and had to pick sides and Austin was there, he would be my first choice. Austin could play anywhere in the backs, scrum-half, stand-off, full-back. If push came to shove he could have played on the wing, but he wasn't really fast enough for that – with respect, of course. But he could fill in anywhere and he wouldn't let anyone down.

In the late 1950s and early 1960s, Alex Murphy and Wilf Smith were the half-back pairing and he was full-back in the Championship Final in 1959 and Challenge Cup Final in 1961. But I have to say that I have so much respect for him as a player and as a person. He used to call me the 'Boot.' Before training we used to try and kick goals from all angles. Funnily enough, I would put them over and he couldn't. One day at Featherstone, Austin was on the wing with an ankle injury and there was the chance of a goalkick right under the sticks. He said to Vince Karalius "Give it to the Boot." Anyhow, my attempt was so bad I nearly knocked the corner flag over. I know he will certainly write about it in this book.

They were great days, though, when I was scoring all those tries and Austin was top of the kicking charts. I was so proud of our achievements. I used to say to him that I'd scored under the sticks just to make his kick easier. It developed into some good natured banter between us. If I scored in the corner it was a case of "Jeez, you could have done better than that."

Leonie and I became good friends with Austin and Marlene too, which is still the case today.

Long may it continue.

Tom van Vollenhoven
St Helens RLFC 1957 to 1968

Appendix: Statistics and records

Club, individual and representative record 1955 to 1969

St Helens
Debut versus Liverpool City (H) 28 March 1955 Won 12–4

Season	App	T	G	Pts	Positions played
1954–55	5	1	0	3	SO5
1955–56	38	10	138	306	SO38
1956–57	41	25	145	365	SO14 SH27
1957–58	28	11	91	215	RC4 LC5 SO17 SH8
1958–59	10	4	30	72	FB2 RC1 LC3 SO2 SH2
1959–60	38	19	170	397	FB29 RC1 LC2 SO6
1960–61	39	13	139	317	FB28 RC3 LC2 SO6
1961–62	30	7	87	54	FB20 RC1 LC5 SO4

Honours
1955–56 Challenge Cup winner
1956–57 Lancashire Cup runner-up
1957–58 Lancashire Cup runner-up
1958–59 Lancashire Cup runner-up
1958–59 League Championship winner
1959–60 Lancashire Cup runner-up
1959–60 Lancashire League winner
1960–61 Lancashire Cup winner
1960–61 Challenge Cup winner
1961–62 Lancashire Cup winner

Leigh
Debut versus St Helens (H) 15 September 1962 Lost 20–10

Season	App	T	G	Pts	Positions played
1962–63	18	0	37	74	FB6 LC3 SO6 SH3
1963–64	36	5	13	41	FB3 LC3 RC1 SO29
1964–65	27	4	1	14	FB3 RC1 SO3 SH20

Honours
1963–64 Lancashire Cup runner-up

Swinton
Debut versus Hull KR (A) 21 August 1965 Won 16–15

Season	App	T	G	Pts	Positions played
1965-66	35	3	13	43	RC1 SO33 SH1
1966-67	32	2	2	10	LC1 SO29 SH2
1967-68	20	2	0	6	SO17 SH3

St Helens (Reprise)

Season	App	T	G	Pts	Positions played
1967-68	14	2	7	20	SO12
1968-69	22+8	5	8	31	FB16 SO4 SH2

Honours
1968–69 Lancashire Cup winner
1968–69 Lancashire League winner

Great Britain

Test Match 104 (World Cup)
Great Britain 21 New Zealand 29
25 June 1957 at Sydney Cricket Ground
Rhodes played stand-off

Test Match 121 (World Cup)
Great Britain 33 France 7
1 October 1960 at Station Road, Swinton
Rhodes played right centre; scored two tries

Test Match 122 (World Cup)
Great Britain 10 Australia 3
8 October 1960 at Odsal Stadium, Bradford
Rhodes played full-back; kicked two goals

Representative friendly
Great Britain 33 The Rest 27
10 October 1960 at Odsal Stadium, Bradford
Rhodes played full-back; kicked three goals

Test Match 125
Great Britain 11 New Zealand 29
30 September 1961 at Headingley, Leeds
Rhodes played full-back; kicked a goal

Lancashire

County Championship
Lancashire 11 Yorkshire 25
23 September 1957 at Naughton Park, Widnes
Rhodes played scrum-half

County Championship
Cumberland 14 Lancashire 8
31 August 1959 at Derwent Park, Workington
Rhodes played full-back and kicked a goal

Other representative matches

The 1957 World Cup squad played the following matches after the competition was completed:

Queensland 5 British XIII 44
Representative friendly
1 July 1957 at Lang Park, Brisbane
Rhodes played at stand-off and scored a try and kicked two goals

British XIII 26 French XIII 12
Representative friendly
6 July 1957 at Carlaw Park, Auckland
Rhodes played stand-off and scored a try

British XIII 61 French XIII 41
Representative friendly
20 July 1957 at Willmore Park, Benoni, South Africa
Rhodes played stand-off and scored three tries

British XIII 32 French XIII 11
Representative friendly
24 July 1957 at Kingsmead, Durban, South Africa
Rhodes played stand-off and scored a try

British XIII 69 French XIII 11
Representative friendly
27 July 1957 at Jan Smuts Ground, East London, South Africa
Rhodes played stand-off and scored three tries

Coaching

Swinton:
June 1974 to November 1975
1974-75: Promoted from the Second Division in fourth place.

Pilkington Recs:
1976 to 1978
1976–77: Lancashire and Cumbria County Cup winners
1977–78: Lancashire and Cumbria County Cup winners
1977–78: North West Counties Premier League Champions

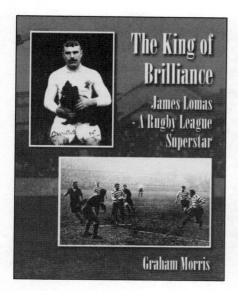

Great new book about one of the sport's genuine legends. James Lomas played for Bramley, Salford, Oldham and York, and won representative honours for Lancashire, Cumberland, England and Great Britain. He captained the first Lions team to tour Australia and New Zealand in 1910. This is the first biography of him.

Published in October 2011 at £16.95 (hardback). Copies available direct from London League Publications Ltd, PO Box 65784, London NW2 9NS (cheques payable to London League Publications Ltd); credit card orders via our website: www.llpshop.co.uk or from any bookshop

Rugby's Greatest Mystery
Who really was F.S. Jackson?

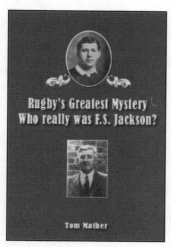

A true life rugby detective story

This is the story of a man whose life was made up of mystery, intrigue and deception, but was also a Rugby Union star before the First World War. He played for Leicester and Cornwall when they won the 1908 County Championship. He was selected for the Anglo-Welsh Rugby Union tour to New Zealand and Australia in 1908. However, the RFU recalled him from the tour and banned him from the sport over allegations that he was a professional player, and had played for Swinton in the Northern Union. The scandal around his suspension from rugby union caused great problems for the RFU and almost saw a further split in the game.

He then played Rugby League for New Zealand, against the British Lions in 1910. After the First World War he was reinstated by the New Zealand RU, became an East Coast selector and saw his son play for the All Blacks. For around 60 years he used the name Frederick Stanley Jackson, even though it was not his given name. When he died in 1957 he took to the grave his true identity. Even his family knew little about his early years in England, or even where he came from. **It was a mystery that remained unresolved until now.** The book also includes an analysis of the development of Leicester Tigers RFC up to the First World War.

Published in March 2012 at £12.95. Copies available direct from
London League Publications Ltd, PO Box 65784, London NW2 9NS
(cheques payable to London League Publications Ltd);
credit card orders via our website: www.llpshop.co.uk or from any bookshop.

Best in the Northern Union

The pioneering 1910
Rugby League Lions tour
of Australia and New Zealand

Tom Mather

Fascinating account of the first Great Britain Lions tour of Australia and New Zealand. Published in 2010 at £12.95, special offer £12.00 direct from London League Publications Ltd. Credit card orders via www.llpshop.co.uk , orders by cheque to LLP, PO Box 65784, London NW2 9NS

Braver than all the rest
A mother fights for her son

Philip Howard

Dave and Sarah Burgess are devastated when their young son Karl is found to
have muscular dystrophy. Then another tragedy hits the family hard. But the
family are committed to do the best they can for Karl, who has a passion for
rugby league. Based in Castleton, a Yorkshire town near the border with
Lancashire, Karl's determination to get the most out of life, despite his
disability, inspires those around him, in particular Chris Anderton, one of the
Castleton Rugby League Club players, who is coming to the end of his career in
the game. A moving novel of family life and rugby league.
Published in 2010 at £9.95, special offer £9.00 direct from London League
Publications Ltd. Credit card orders via www.llpshop.co.uk , orders by cheque
to LLP, PO Box 65784, London NW2 9NS

153

From grass to glass

A Rugby League Journey

Paul Loughlin

with Andrew Quirke

Autobiography of Great Britain, St Helens, Huddersfield and Bradford Bulls Star.
Published in 2011 at £12.95, special offer £12.00 direct from London League
Publications Ltd. Credit card orders via www.llpshop.co.uk ,orders by cheque to
LLP, PO Box 65784, London NW2 9NS